Behaviorism and Schooling

Behaviorism and Schooling

IRA S. STEINBERG

Oberlin College

ST. MARTIN'S • NEW YORK

ISBN 0-312-07253-8

Library of Congress Cataloging in Publication Data

Steinberg, Ira S
  Behaviorism and schooling.

  Bibliography: p.
  1.   Learning, Psychology of.   2.   Students —
Psychology.   3.   Behaviorism (Psychology)   I.   Title.
LB1051.S71256   1980   370.15   80-13602
ISBN 0-312-07253-8

for
Uncle Mel

Contents

Acknowledgments

My thanks to all who contributed to the publication of this book. Oberlin College provided funds to assist in the preparation of the manuscript. Discussion with colleagues in the Department of Philosophy helped to sharpen my thinking on the topics included. Wendy Looman typed the first draft. April Paramore and Nancy Schwarzwalder typed the final draft. My wife, Priscilla, provided support and encouragement at the expense of her summer holiday.

Behaviorism and Schooling

CHAPTER 1

Schooling and Behaviorism: The Art and the Science of Utopia

Long before recorded time people, or whatever we were before we were really people, had been learning from and teaching one another all sorts of things in various ways. For humans, survival of the species, the group, the individual has always depended upon learning and teaching that which does not come instinctively. The development of even the most uncomplicated culture by current standards requires the passing over to the young of the particular modes of living peculiar to a given group. At the very least, there must be imitation by the young of activities of their elders. Successful imitation requires apprehension of the details of what is to be imitated. Teaching, again at the very least as the encouragement or imposition of imitation, requires the same. Here is the source of our most primitive conceptions of behaviorism, of schooling and of their connection.

Assuming that most of us know and have read quite a lot about schooling, I have chosen to concentrate my efforts in this work on an examination of behaviorism and its connection with schooling. Still, I owe the reader some account of what I have in mind in my use of that term. Roughly, it amounts to this.

There appears to be an almost universal concern that young people receive appropriate instruction in the basic skills of literacy at least, and that they should learn the basic rudiments of mathematics, the natural sciences, history and the like. The responsibility for the provision of such instruction lies with the body politic, through the appropriate agencies of government. Whatever else one might mean by education, there are some educational tasks to be performed, there are some things children are to be taught, in an organized and efficient manner in formal settings called schools. Schooling may include a number of different subjects or interests. The tasks may be interpreted more or less broadly. There may be opportunities for all manner of accidental or incidental learning. But, at its core it is a purposeful business. There is a reason to insist that children should be in school. That reason is that there are some things which they ought to be taught and which they ought to know and this shall not be left to chance.

Now, a few disclaimers are in order to make clear what I do not have in mind by schooling. First, in giving this general account, I do not intend to suggest that private or church schooling is somehow illegitimate. There was a time and there are yet places where schooling is or was taken to be the prerogative of family or church. It is a safe reflection of general opinion now that at the very least the state, in the general interest, should insist on some form of schooling up to some adjudged standard and provide state schools for those who do not avail themselves of private or church schools.

Second, in providing an example of rather widespread concern for literacy I am not defining schooling by necessary content or subjects of instruction. The point is that schooling entails the idea that some things need to be taught and learned by new members of a society. What these things are may differ from society to society. Within a given society they may differ for groups or classes of individuals (in the sense that they have in fact so differed beyond some very low minimum). The more complex the culture of a given society, the more heterogeneous the interests, backgrounds and occupations of its members, the more likely that there might be controversy and changes in public opinion about what the central tasks of schooling 'really are,' though agreement that there are central or common tasks may remain undiminished.

Third, the idea that schooling is purposeful in endeavoring to see to it that children learn what they are supposed to learn is not in itself to endorse any particular approach to teaching. Efficiency is not guaranteed by the unthinking adoption of particular teaching methods. To insist that children go to school to learn particular things rather than leaving that learning to chance without schooling does not mean that everything can be taught or learned in school 'by the numbers', as it were. The test of efficiency is in the effect of technique. Perhaps a good many things are best learned in school through rather free-ranging inquiry on the part of children.

Finally, and following on this last observation, schooling cannot in its purposiveness guarantee success. Perhaps there are some things that we do not know how to teach in school. Perhaps there are some things that we do not know how to teach to some people. At its best, schooling only promises to try its best to teach what it is instituted to teach. At its worst it pretends to do so. But schooling is no easy business, nor has it ever been so.

Behavior and Schooling: The Pre-Scientific Tradition

Two and a half millenia ago Plato raised the most crucial questions of education. (In the dialogue of that name) *Meno* asked Socrates whether virtue is taught or whether it comes to us as a gift of nature or of the gods. Characteristically, Socrates asked in reply what virtue is, for how, he wondered can we know whether it is taught, if we are not clear about what it is? Considering the differences among the various conceptions of virtue from Socratic times to the present day, we too may wonder what it is the schools are to accomplish when we press upon them the noble task of ennobling the future citizenry. And like Socrates we too may ask, as he did of Meno, whether anyone really does know how to teach virtue. Is there any good evidence or example to show that the presumed teachers of virtue do, indeed, turn out virtuous students. Is there any reason to believe that the prime examples of special virtue have any more luck than the rest of mankind in raising their children to be virtuous? Socrates found none. He ended the dialogue more or less forced to conclude that virtue comes by some sort of divine dispensation. He was unsure about this because he was unsure about the nature of virtue itself.

The *Meno* ended here, in uncertainty, perhaps even in confusion. Yet the central issues of the nature of knowledge and belief — of meaning, of evidence, of social stability and responsibility, of morality (so many issues), of philosophy in general — had been introduced as bearing on the question of the teaching of virtue. Plato's concern for this question might have ended here, with the implication that reliance on divine dispensation was all that men had going for them in ensuring the representation of virtue in succeeding generations. But Plato was very much concerned for virtue in society. That concern led to the first comprehensive treatise on schooling in western literature, *The Republic.*

Of course *The Republic* was more than a treatise on schooling. Its ostensible focus was on the explication of the meaning of justice and a demonstration that the just life was to be preferred over the unjust life. Plato, in the character of Socrates, developed a sketch of an ideal society: its economy, social structure and political structure. He presented us with an outline of the nature of the ideal citizen or leader of such a society, the so-called philosopher king. He also outlined a theory of knowledge that requires philosophers to be kings. Schooling was essential to the development and maintenance of the ideal society: the fitting of the citizenry for their roles, their duties and stations in society.

Plato indulged in a bit of armchair social science and armchair psychology in talking about the proper character of society and the proper character of the individual person. In fact he seems to have got these two sorts of entity thoroughly mixed together for purposes of 'scientific' methodology and philosophical explanation. He set about explaining justice in the individual by looking for it in the larger plan of the state. The ideal state is led by the wisest, protected by the bravest who yet know enough to follow the wise, and supported by the majority of people as they go about the business of supplying everyday needs and wants — the necessary appetites. Even the last know enough to follow the dictates of reason. The state, in fact, was presented on analogy with the rational man who controls his potential for violent or vigorous action and his appetites as dictated by a reasoned concern for his overall well-being. In turn the ideal sort of personality is one that is ruled as the ideal state is ruled. The state was in fact modeled after the ideal individual: the man or woman (Plato was ahead of his time even in this) in whom the capacity for reason was greatest *and* best developed, yet who was no less courageous than the most courageous and still had the normal urges and appetites. The notion of justice was pretty much embodied in the recognition by all people that things should be so ordered in the individual and in the state that each element of the soul or the body politic did his/its proper thing in accordance with his/its nature.

Now, I am not at all concerned here to sell or defend Plato's conception of the ideal state. Nor am I here concerned especially to attack it. Rather I wish to emphasize the technique of modeling the state on the analogy of the characterology of the individual. In the section on the demise of the ideal state, Plato spoke about the effects of social competition and class on the shaping of the personality of the young. Then in each stage of decline from the most ideal to the most corrupt form of state he described the state by analogy with its corresponding characteristic citizen. It is not always clear whether he is defining the nature of different sorts of states by reference to certain personalities, thereby engaging in personification (e.g., as when democracy is ruled by appetites and passions), or is ascribing the changes to the action of individuals with certain character traits (as when a man with mixed motives is led first one way and then another by his sense of honor or self-interest as he is tugged upon by esteem and flattery). This sort of armchair social science/psychology and analogy from the individual to the body politic has dominated what we might call pre-scientific social science ever since Plato.

Unlike all too many armchair theorists, Plato had a healthy regard for the limits of theory. In *The Republic* he set out to show that a certain type of state was feasible — it could exist. He tried to show what it would take to make it work and how it might work for a time. But its continuation required omniscience and absolute incorruptibility of the leadership. These he would not grant.

If education or schooling was essential to the development and maintenance of the ideal state, it was so as a necessary, but not as a sufficient, condition. Schooling was fundamentally concerned with two things. First was the development of appropriate beliefs on the part of the citizenry at large — beliefs (moral, esthetic, patriotic, etc.) conducive to loyalty to the ideal society and one's place in it. Second, was the selection out of the mass and creaming off in stages of the military and ultimately the ruling class. Basic character, intelligence, drive, etc. were innate — genetically endowed. Education could develop that character, intelligence, drive, but it could not create them. Errors would ultimately be made in the selection of members of the ruling class. Flawed character allied to superior intellect would lead the state down the slope of decline.

It is with respect to schooling that Plato seems more an empiricist in outlook. He does say some rather odd things about the likely effects of certain sorts of poetry on personality formation or about the dramatic portrayal of females by boys making them effeminate.

This is armchair empiricism at its worst. Still, he is very much committed to the basic behavioral conditioning position of providing only those models of behavior that one wants adopted and of fitting our educational expectations to the behavioral capabilities of people at different ages. His attention to the details of the life-style of the ruling class underlines his concern to reinforce by environment and structure the lessons of schooling. It is one thing to teach the young that they should not wish for luxury or material possessions; it is another to initiate them into an ongoing way of life which has no room for such luxury and replaces material gain with honorifics. Finally, in emphasizing selection in education, Plato did not presume that he could make anyone anything he might will. On the contrary, he showed a healthy empiricism with respect to the limits of what the teacher might do given the human material with which he had to work.

In *The Republic,* Plato identified schooling with the enterprise of deliberate fitting of the young for society. The critique of schooling required a clear understanding of the nature and character of people, the nature and structure of society, the relationship of culture to society, and the nature of human development. In addition, it was to proceed through the provision of activities and setting of tasks increasingly more demanding in fortitude and intellect required for their accomplishment, selecting individuals for the various levels of social role on the basis of performance. Moreover, if one is concerned, as Plato was, to restructure — to reform — society, then one should note as well Plato's recognition of the limits of the power of schooling. Society must be restructured along with the redesign of schooling. Plato did not seem very optimistic about the potential of schooling as the instrument of social reform in the absence of control of the political, social, and, indeed, the child-rearing parental structure. The institutions and practices of society must be such as to reinforce schooling. To be selected for a place in a structure requires that the structure exists so that one can take one's place. A set of beliefs, an outlook on life, a morality, at odds with those held and expressed generally in society or by those in position to lead opinion, are not likely to be instilled successfully in the majority of the young or to survive their schooling unalloyed.

Now, there are people who believe that the means to the reform or reconstruction of society is through education. If one could somehow alter what people are taught and how they are taught we could create a generation of new men and women who would construct a society consistent with their best developed natures. Leaping lightly over a couple of thousand years from ancient Athens we find the prime spokesman for this view in *ancien régime* France. Writing in the twilight of the old order and the dawn of modern behavioral science and fitting comfortably with neither was Jean Jacques Rousseau.

Rousseau thoroughly detested the society of his day. He opposed the principle of absolutism in the monarchy but was not opposed to monarchy as such. He did not think that a pure democracy was consistent with the nature of man, but tended to favor some sort of government by election of the best sort from among the citizenry at large, provided that the citizenry was not too large. He suspected large political entities, favoring smaller nation-states and sub-states. He detested most of all over-sophistication in culture: the fragmentation of the mainly self-sufficient man in the nuclear family cooperating with others for their mutual protection turned into the specialist producer of luxuries of no real use to the wholesome support of human society.

He too would study human nature and human society as the armchair psychologist/anthropologist. He would leave man educated in accordance with his nature to alter that nature as little as possible, but sufficient to make him a moral, civil being, self-reliant in his knowledge and capabilities but cognizant of his obligations to society as the price of society's obligations to him. But he was to be educated to be a citizen of society as it ought to be and to recognize the need to come to terms with civil society even if less than ideal. He might have as little as possible to do with a corrupt society but he would not live outside society.

The standards of education for Rousseau, as for Plato, were to be found in the ideal view of society, human nature, human development, culture and their relationships. Education for Rousseau, as for Plato, was a fundamentally behavioristic enterprise. Indeed nowhere has this position been more strongly urged than in the instructions to the tutor in *Emile*:

Is not this poor child without knowledge, strength, or wisdom, entirely at your mercy? Are you not master of his environment so far as it affects him? Cannot you make of him what you please? His work and play, his pleasure and pain, are they not, unknown to him, under your control? No doubt he ought only to do what he wants, but he ought to want to do nothing but what you want him to do. He should never take a step you have not foreseen, nor utter a word you could not foretell. [pp. 84-5]

Again like Plato, Rousseau was very much an armchair empiricist with respect to education. One should evaluate the content and the process of schooling by reference to effects, but somehow Rousseau seemed to be able to discover effects without having to observe them. He called upon his own experience and reasoning. He spoke the language of empiricism and operated in the rationalist mode.

Now, the perceptive reader may have noticed an equivocation in the foregoing comparison of Plato and Rousseau. Whereas I spoke about Plato's views on *schooling,* I have spoken of Rousseau's views on *education.* One can (in the *Social Contract*) find support for an instituted education (i.e., schooling). Rousseau in *Emile* is adamantly opposed to the idea in his commitment to the sanctity of the family and the primacy of the father's responsibility to educate his son. (The mother could provide the upbringing appropriate to a woman for her daughter — Rousseau was not so enlightened as Plato with respect to the equality of men and women.) Where the father cannot educate his son himself, he must engage a tutor whose sole occupation is to raise the child to manhood. Plato would redesign the state and the man. Rousseau would redesign the man to make his own state. Plato, it happens, was fearful of anarchy leading to despotism; Rousseau, of absolutism and the tyranny of excessive social organization. Plato sought order in society under the rule of reason. Rousseau sought freedom for the individual from interference in the exercise of his common sense in support of his own and his family's well-being.

Somehow the impracticability of Rousseau's program of education (after all how could one supply each person in society with a live-in tutor for twenty years or so) has become converted or subverted over the years to the general commitment to schooling. The schools are so to educate the young as to prepare them to reform society. The schools are to change society. Rousseau would never have believed it. Plato would scarcely have given the idea a chance. And yet this is the cornerstone of modern educational faith. It is the source of great mischief. It is intended to prevent great mischief. It is most confusing.

Schooling should be deliberate in the design of activities to fit the young for the sort of society that they shall deem appropriate as they create that society. This provides us with a criterion for the evaluation of educational policy and practice that sounds impressive but is literally unintelligible. Those who must educate the young can never claim to know at any given time whether their policies and practices are currently in line with such a criterion. The criterion can only be applied in hindsight, if at all, by those who have been educated and it can only be applied to their own past education. For, as they would educate their children they cannot know what sort of society their children will construct. The criterion is no criterion at all. It permits no particular policy or practice of schooling and it prohibits none. Yet it appears to do both. This encourages a sort of scholasticism in the effort to find justifiable practice and policy. It leads to partisanship and contention over who has captured truth in such matters.

And yet it is intended to prevent another sort of mischief. There is a great distrust that schooling might be too purposeful, too efficient in suiting the young for the new society. There is the fear that those who can control schooling as the agency of the state may impose on the young the wrong conception of an ideal society or a narrowly conceived, insufficiently humane, or overly authoritarian or a totalitarian conception of society. The vision of schooling as an education to fit each generation to create society anew, while quite vague as to program and content, is intended to protect the continuing freedom and autonomy of successive generations from the imposition of anyone's vision of the ideal society. It uses the language of reform for the prevention of reform and is, indeed, thereby confusing.

This confusion in contemporary thinking about schooling and social reform as societal reconstruction has its roots in the sorts of concerns expressed most fundamentally by Plato and Rousseau, but they did not convert these concerns into the confusion. For that to happen it took, among other things, the development of modern social science.

The Quest for a Science of Man

The roots of modern social science are many and tangled. The historic and traditional philosophic concern for social reform and reconstruction — the development of an ideal society with its attendant intellectual demands for understanding the nature of man and human and social development — had been expressed in a number of ways over the centuries. The rise of organized religion and the development of theology intertwined with varied conceptions of the nature of man and of God and of knowledge and of reality. The concern of philosophers especially with knowledge and reality ultimately gave rise to the liberation of natural science from the dictates of religious orthodoxy.

The development of the idea that one can find knowledge about things in nature in the ordinary way of looking and supposing and checking one's suppositions by more looking — the rise of empiricism — has a long tradition. This idea was certainly alive in the time of the ancients. It was eclipsed by rationalism in one form or another and in one theological system or another which sought to make the Realm of God in his heavens more real than the Realm of man on earth. The heroes who brought science out of the shadows from the fifteenth century on are well known — Copernicus, Bacon, Galileo, *et al.* But it was with Newton in the seventeenth century that modern natural science had arrived.[1]

Newton had an impact far beyond his direct contribution to physical theory. In explaining the operations of the heavens and of the earth in the same mathematically formulable laws he reversed the order of explanation of received theological systems and undercut rationalism. One was not to explain the natural workings of things by what seemed reasonable to imagine as God's will or what seemed self-evident to reason. Rather one began with what appeared to the senses as given and sought to discover the regularities of nature and to calculate those regularities. To find the constants of nature, the constant relationship among events, this was to explain. Of course, this was not a blind empiricism of observation, supposition, and testing of one's hypotheses. It represented a marriage of the outlook and ultimate ground of empiricism with the formal technique of rationalism — logical, mathematical reasoning — in the development of theoretical physics. Common sense surely had difficulty with the magic of action at a distance in the operations of natural magnets (lodestone). To see objects falling to the earth as the same sort of thing as the attraction of the planets — such disparate things acting on one another without touching — this was surely beyond the ordinary conception of observation. And yet the calculations seemed to hold.

The 'incomparable Newton' Locke called him. And Locke sailed into Cartesian rationalism determined to replace Descartes' conception of how we understand the world with a thoroughgoing empiricism. Our ideas do not come originally from within but from the world out there. For Locke, Newton was the ideological emancipator. Locke was not a physicist. He was a philosopher. No matter whether Newton thought himself a metaphysician. For Locke he had provided the true First Philosophy. Through Locke, his followers and critics in England and in France, empiricism was promoted as the means of human knowledge and as the means of understanding man and how he knows things. If received religion held to a hierarchy of the kingdom of God, the kingdom of Man and the Animal kingdom, Newton placed heaven and earth in the same plane of nature. If man was not yet God, he could be examined and understood as an animal.

By the end of the eighteenth century and especially in France the search was on for a 'Mechanics of Human Behavior' and a 'Physics of Society'.[2] The physiological analogy of man and the higher animals had long since been documented. What was important in materialism, what was important for *Les ideologues,* was that, given the parallel physiology, human behavior should be explained and predicted in much the same way as animal behavior and furthermore that the source of behavior lies in the adaptation and interaction of the animal with his environment. There is even the anticipation of Darwin's *Descent of Man* in the notion that man must have his roots in the development from the primates. If man was more than an ape with clothing, he was at least that.

In what sense was man more than an ape? He had language. His behavior was more complex. He had moral sensibilities. But for some, at least, all this was a matter of degree. Animals communicated by signs and engaged in rather complex activities. If one has ever seen a sheepdog working a flock from one pasture to another or a pair of dogs coordinating their moves in a hunt, one is readily convinced of this. Animals have moral sensibilities on this view; pets show gratitude, affection, responsibility and the like to one another and to the members of the family that keeps them. And examples can be found in nature, uninfluenced by man's domestication, of similar qualities. Moreover, just as animals learn to communicate by signs, to do all sorts of things to develop their sensibilities, so too in the same way does man. In the words of La Mettrie:

Words, languages, laws, sciences, and the fine arts have come, and by them finally the rough diamond of our mind has been polished. Man has been trained in the same way as animals. He has become an author, as they became beasts of burden. A geometrician has learned to perform the most difficult demonstrations and calculations, as a monkey has learned to take his hat off and on, and to mount his tame dog. All has been accomplished through signs, every species has learned what it could understand, and in this way men have acquired symbolic knowledge . . .

But who was the first to speak? Who was the first teacher of the human race? Who invented the means of utilizing the plasticity of our organism? I can not answer: the names of these splended geniuses have been lost in the night of time. But art is the child of nature, so nature must have long preceeded it. [1748, pp. 103-4]

Here is a statement of foundation for the scientific study of man. Human nature is a part of nature at large; the laws of human nature are to be found in the laws of nature. Human behavior is determined by the same laws that determine all behavior. Indeed, while La Mettrie was prepared to endow animals with human-like thoughts and feelings and even free will, other writers went quite the other way. If animals are not to be granted symbolized thought, moral sentiments, and free will, if animal behavior is determined by the natural constitution of the animal interacting with its environment, then so too is human behavior determined. We have no need for the notion of free will in explaining the behavior of the physical universe. Why, then, should we need such a notion in explaining the behavior of animals in that universe, even of animals such as man? The laws of behavior should be, on this view, as deterministic as the laws of physics.

Moreover, on this view one can dispense with the notion of morality. Where there is no free will, there is no possibility of moral or immoral behavior. There is only behavior of organisms in accordance with their natures in response to environmental conditions in conformity with the laws of nature. We may judge some behavior as good or bad, as fortunate or unfortunate in its effects, but not as moral or immoral. As one can see, the view that man is a creature of forces and conditions beyond his control is not all that new even in its supposed scientific dress. As we can see, the source of the mistrust of a science of human nature as dehumanizing man is not new either. For, what sort of *human* nature is it in which morality has no place? How can one understand human nature as human if there is no place for free will in that understanding?

Nevertheless, out of this attitude toward human nature came a new impetus for the reform and reconstruction of society, only this time in scientific terms. Here are the roots of the Saint-Simonian utopian socialisms and the science and religion of positivism of Auguste Comte in the early nineteenth century.[3] Given the plasticity or adaptability of man's physiological/intellectual endowment, his capacity to learn as emphasized by La Mettrie. Given the faith in the existence of deterministic laws of human nature/behavior as emphasized by Holbach. Given the peculiar notion that the natural tends to the good (La Mettrie, perhaps a throwback to Rousseau). Or given, instead, the equally peculiar notion that the nature of man defines his well-being — that there is a natural healthy social-cultural state of man. Or even, given the idea that man lacking free will and morality may yet live a good life as defined by some men, at least. Then it behoves us to discover those laws of nature, to develop the technology of influencing learning and human behavior and so to order the environment (that is to say the social environment) of man as to develop that society in which man might best thrive. The utopian socialists would, in good Rousseauian fashion (indeed even good Platonic fashion), peel away the layers of unnecessary custom, luxury, bureaucracy, to the essential social institutions. Comte would call for a physics of society to discover the technology and the science of human progress through social organization. He would seek the laws of social organization. And he would replace the religion of God with a secular religion of man, the rewards of enduring life in heaven for the virtuous replaced by enshrinement in the memory of the people for contribution to the well-being of mankind.

The enthusiasm with which such writers argued for the advancement of a science of human nature and of society may be judged in the strength of this language, the scope and detail of the matters they covered and their prolific written output. Still, an argument for a science is not yet a science, and by that standard they were rather long on promise and short on accomplishment. What they did seem to accomplish is of mixed blessing. They translated the historic, traditional concern for social reform and reconstruction into the language of modern scientific thought. If they were the precursors of modern social science, they were also the fathers of scientism in social thought. In promising so much and delivering so little they fostered a skepticism regarding the prospects of social science among ordinary intellectuals, but especially among natural scientists, that has endured to the present day. Their very utopianism, their social meliorism, in presuming, on scientific grounds now, to organize society in the best interests of individuals, 'in spite of themselves' or to make of them their better selves, continues to raise suspicion among those of an independent responsibility, moral agency of man, civil libertarian bent. Only, now, that suspicion is converted to a suspicion of the motivation of social scientists and the likely scientific neutrality or objectivity of social science. In placing the perfectability of man in society in the future development of social science they, or at least Comte, converted the philosopher king of Plato into the positive scientist. Even more, as modern science took as its goal the advancement of knowledge, a progressive increase in and knowledge of the world, positivism proposed not the static ideal society of Plato's *Republic,* but the improving society progressing with the advancement of and understanding of human nature and the social physics. Science promises progress toward an end without the end in view, progress toward an ever-changing end. Here is the anticipation, if you will, of the pragmatism of the late nineteenth and early twentieth century under the influence of which in the United States, at least, modern social science came of age.

Pragmatism emerged in the latter third of the nineteenth century as a reassertion of common sense realism and commitment to the spirit of empirical science in intellectual and practical affairs. For C. S. Peirce, the father of American pragmatism, the enemies were obscurantism and authoritarianism in philosophy and theology.[4] The nineteenth century had seen a reassertion of rationalism in one form or another: a resurgence of idealism, that peculiar doctrine that existence depends on cognition whether of men or some absolute being; a revival of fundamentalist religious doctrine and faith in the literal biblical account of the creation of the universe and everything in it; and, in general, all manner of beliefs inconsistent with the advancement of scientific thinking. And yet this was the age of the industrial revolution, the application of science through technology and an empirical point of view to the restructuring of economic life and especially the redesign and reorganization of the production of goods *en masse* and the creation and servicing of mass markets. This was the age of rugged individualism, of the ruthless entrepreneur out to establish a neo-feudalism based on the barony of accumulated industrial capital. They were not without apologists — Herbert Spencer and William Graham Sumner were chief among them — eager to expound the doctrine that it was a law of God and of nature that the fittest should survive. Social Darwinism it has been called.[5]

The harbingers of Darwin had ultimately been forgotten in the scope and comprehensive nature of his magnificent accomplishment in *The Origin of the Species* published in 1859. So too had their concern for the restructuring of society for the advancement of the human species as such. For Darwinism came to mean a translation of the old Protestant Ethic, and especially the idea of evidencing divine grace in earthly accomplishment, into the notion that a society's advance was to be accomplished in and measured by the success of those of its members best fitted to succeed. Those lesser creatures unfit to make do in the world did not deserve to make do. Their failure to survive only served to 'cull the flock' of the weakest and improve the breeding stock for the future. The fact that it was man feeding on man for his success was understood or explained away by analogy with the flock or herd or pack eliminating its own weaklings. The inhumanity of man preying on man, the rise of industrial society with its great wealth for a few and increasing concentration for many in squalid mill towns, and even more squalid burgeoning cities, had turned Rousseau's ideal of the society of independent self-sufficient families on its head.

In response to the industrialization of poverty, with increasing urbanization of society and, in the United States, with the waves of increasing immigration aggravating these problems, there arose a concern for reform and reconstruction of society. The so-called Progressive movement at the turn of the century was a mixed bag. There were the sort of humane do-gooders with specific concerns about eliminating child-labor and improving working conditions, especially for women. There were those who worried about the shock of entry into a new culture for the immigrant, though, more often, there was concern to assimilate the immigrant to protect American society from his ignorance and/or Eastern or Southern European or Irish, etc., sloth and depravity. There were those who wished to reform schooling. There were those who would have laws passed to limit the empire building of the industrial giants and 'bust the trusts'. There were also some who would advance the scientific study of the economy, of social structure, of industrial organization, of the culture of the immigrant, of urbanization, etc. The impetus for such study grew out of the concern for dealing with social problems: the problems had to be understood if they were to be dealt with.[6]

The prime source of the scientific attitude toward such study appears to have been Peirce and pragmatism. William James at Harvard and John Dewey at Chicago and Columbia universities were the apostles of pragmatism. They preached their own versions of it; indeed Peirce sought to disencumber his position from theirs (Buchler, 1955, pp. 251-89). Still they broadcast a concern for social reform and social justice, the application of the scientific method to the understanding of the nature of man and of society and with Dewey, especially, the reform of society through the reform of schooling. Pragmatism for Dewey, as for G. H. Mead, represented the quest for what would work, what would be valuable, what would prove to be true (Scheffler, 1974). In its social form, it was a commitment to construct a society in search of its own improvement. If our understanding of the universe was always changing, always in progress, then our reconstruction of society must always be in progress. The schools must instill this attitude and the commitment to the cooperation of all for the benefit of all in the society of all. It was in this spirit that the various social sciences and psychology were being established as separate disciplines at that time. The students of James and Dewey and Mead were to establish empirical sciences of psychology and sociology, emphasizing, on the one hand, the experimental mode of observation and, on the other, the careful, thorough gathering and organization of data. The sciences of man and society had come out of the armchair and into the laboratory, the factory, the neighborhood.

Experimental psychology reaffirmed the continuity of the natural order, placing man in nature in the quest for the laws of learning. Wilhelm Wundt is generally credited with the establishment of the development of psychology through attention to animal behavior. But, E. L. Thorndike set the pattern of experimental psychological research that is still dominant in the field to this date: extrapolation from controlled manipulation of animal behavior to the generalization of the grounds of behavior in general, including human behavior. His laws of learning, his account of stimulus and response, were to undergo various modifications and interpretations within the field over the course of the century, but the central core remained intact. It was no less than a restatement of the position of the core of French materialism — of La Mettrie, *et al.* What a man is, what a man knows, believes, thinks, feels, these represent the connection between his nature (his natural endowment) on the one hand, and his environment (his physical and social context, his experience in the stimuli that impinge upon him) on the other (Joncich, 1962).

It was J. B. Watson, though, who is generally credited as the source of behaviorism in psychology. He too based his work in experimentation with animals. He too had a form of stimulus-response psychology. But he tended to be concerned less with an explanation of mind and more with a rather direct 'excitation of centers of response' approach. Perhaps Thorndike would intellectualize the description of animal behavior to derive general laws suitable as well to humans. Watson would assimilate human behavior to the unthinking response of automata. Watson was also a polemicist with an eye for public attention. Deservedly or not American experimental psychology was tarred with the brush of a rather naive behaviorism (Broadhurst, 1968).

The label was Watson's, but the impact came from Thorndike. That impact was felt perhaps most strongly in the effort to develop a science and technology of schooling. Thorndike wrote early and throughout his career on the importance of understanding the nature of the learner if one is to shape his learning. Psychology was to be the science underlying the technology of schooling. Thorndike proposed a variety of school materials and texts illustrative of his psychological principles. His experiences in the First World War in the design and admission of the army 'alpha' testing of intelligence was to blossom into the psychological testing and evaluation movement in education and ultimately into the identification of science in education with the tested and testable evaluation of achievement — whether of teaching or of learning is still a matter of controversy.

For social reformers like Dewey, schooling is the agency for reform (Dewey, 1899; 1916). The technology of schooling is then the technology of reform and the underlying science of that technology must be the science of social reform, improvement, progress or what have you. The object is to make the Rousseauian ideal come true in twentieth-century terms. If the social structure is bad, again peel away those elements that are bad and so educate the young to design for themselves a truly democratic society where each is the equal of the other and none seeks to use others for his own ends. In the United States the developing behavioral psychology promised reform of society through the remaking of man. So too in the Soviet Union where Dewey's principles were interpreted in the light of scientific materialism. But then modernizing Japan showed an interest in the notion of systematic, scientifically based reformulation of the peasant into the industrial citizen.

Behavioral principles appear to be neutral with respect to the sort of character that individuals are to have and the sort of society they are to form. If, indeed, psychology is to be the ultimate science of social reform, then we must remember that it does not define the necessary or the proper end of reform. It describes at best how learning takes place, perhaps even what sort of things may or may not be learned under what sorts of conditions. It may result in technology that will influence the learning of specific sorts of things rather than other sorts of things that enable us to expect some sorts of behavior rather than other sorts, some attitudes rather than others. But, as science and technology, behaviorism does not tell us for what ends behavior should be shaped.

There is nothing in nature that tells us that each man shall count as one and only one. There is nothing in nature that tells us that all are endowed with the same natural capacities. There is nothing in nature that tells us that those with superior native intelligence should not apply that intelligence to their own self-advancement even at the expense of the less well-advanced. There is nothing in nature that favors democracy over some form of authoritarianism. At least there is nothing of the sort in the nature available to the natural scientist, or the social scientist who would claim the status accorded to the natural scientist. Thorndike clearly believed in the importance of heredity in accounting for individual differences in ability of people. Watson appeared to believe that people could be induced to learn just about anything through appropriate development of behavioral technology. Unfortunately these issues continue to divide people to this day and they figure prominently in the criticism of schooling.

In *The Republic* Plato would educate those with the greatest potential for wisdom and courage to rule in the interest of society at large. Yet we have always had to deal with the problem of ensuring that those most intellectually endowed would have the character to rule and to rule in the interest of society, or that those with the necessary strength of character would have the intelligence or even that those with the appropriate concern for the well-being of society would have the other necessary qualities. Rousseau, recognizing the differences in the natural talents of men, yet believed that men could be educated in such a way and for such a society as would permit them to manage most of their affairs with those talents they held in common. At the very least they were endowed with sense enough to employ the specially talented as needed. Dewey was all too aware of the difference in natural endowment among individuals. His hope was that schooling would provide an opportunity to practice citizenship, behavior that would reinforce cooperation of all for social ends and eliminate the temptation of the most gifted to take advantage of others. More recently, B. F. Skinner would have us so structure society, as well as schooling, that the more talented would run things and each person in society would be reinforced in those attitudes and behaviors conducive to the well-being of society in a society freed from the mythology of freedom and dignity — the behaviorally engineered society (Skinner, 1948; 1971).

If this is too optimistic a view of the potential of behavioral science (though, in a sense, horrifying for some as well), there is an even more optimistic view. This is the view that would deny that there are inherited gifts at all, but claims rather that the differences in men are a matter of environmental advantage whether of class, wealth, or culture. Behaviorism on this account assumes that with appropriate control of environment, with appropriate behavioral technology, all may be brought to similar high standards of accomplishment. The task is to make all equal in wisdom, character, and good will, that all or any may rule. The recurrent tendency to evaluate schooling by reference to the data on testing of pupil performance often appears to take this sort of line. The schools are faulted for not educating all up to some standard of achievement. When teachers and administrators of the schools point out that they have different sorts of students with different sorts of backgrounds in heredity and environment, they are accused of blaming their students for the failures of schooling.

Somehow the measurement of school achievement and of intelligence of the children of varying social classes, ethnic groups or of parents in different occupational categories has become identified as the application of the sophisticated tools of modern behavioral science to the description, definition and solution of modern societal problems through the agency of schooling. If all that behaviorism as the science of schooling can do is to document the differences in achievement of its pupils, then, for social critics of an extreme egalitarian bent, the whole paraphenalia of educational testing is morally suspect. While it does sound a bit like killing the messenger who brings bad news, the messenger may be partly to blame in this case. The very construction of the enterprise of professional and technical expertise in education, the very pretensions to scientific status, the expanding demands for certification of satisfactory professional study and training and of familiarity with the procedures and results of educational research for teachers and administrators, all these have led the public to expect that education can deliver the goods — that enlightened democratic citizenry we promise ourselves to be or become. Behaviorism as science may once again have promised too much. Whether it will, or should survive in spite of this or because of this remains to be seen. But before we return to those questions and with this sort of grand quasi-historical overview introducing the issues now behind us, let us move on to deal with the philosophical issues in behavior and behaviorism in more philosophical fashion.

NOTES

1. For an excellent discussion of the impact of Newton and Locke on the development of a science of man see Berlin (1956).
2. See Potts and Charlton (1972) for an overview of the modern development of French philosophy.
3. For background to Comte and an excellent compendium of his writings see Lenzer (1975).
4. See Scheffler (1974) for discussion of the major figures in American pragmatism.
5. For discussion of Spencer, Sumner and social Darwinism see Hofstadter (1945).
6. See Cremin (1961) for a history of the rise of progressivism, especially in education.

CHAPTER 2

Behavior

As I have characterized things thus far, schooling and behaviorism intersect in their concern with 'behavior'. I will talk about behaviorism in the next chapter (though some discussion of it will be anticipated in this one). First, I want to see if it is perfectly clear just what it is that schooling is supposed to influence when it influences 'behavior'. Just what is it that the behavioral scientist explains, accounts for, predicts, controls, when he studies 'behavior'. What *is* behavior anyhow?

Behavior, in its most general sense, is what people, or animals or even things do. Molecules collide. People collide. Horses perspire. People perspire. Molecules do not. People read and write. People play football. People play the violin. We do indeed apply the term 'behavior' in a most general way.

Perhaps we need to narrow our focus a bit. After all, we are not interested in behavior in general. Our main interest is the behavior of people. Of course we shall have to remind ourselves that behaviorists historically have been concerned to account for human behavior on the same explanatory basis as that of animals. They sought to place the science of man in the science of nature. For now, though, let us just ask 'what is human behavior?'

Well, what sort of things do people do? We do some things that require a good deal of skill. We do some things that require no skill at all. We do some things that require the exercise of intellect. We do other things unthinkingly. We do some things that once took intelligent attention and now can only be performed unthinkingly. (Try running up a flight of stairs while thinking about how to do it.) We do some things as individuals that cannot be done by a group. We do some things as a group that cannot be done individually.

21

Some of us do some things in certain characteristic ways and others do these things in rather different characteristic ways. Perhaps we might best begin our examination of human behavior with the simplest sorts and work our way up the scale of intellectual and social complexity.

Natural Behavior

The infant's first act on arrival into the world is in response to the shock of arrival. He cries. Instinct, the only one we seem to agree on for humans, leads him to suck on the nipple. He performs the usual fundamental bodily functions associated with mammalian life — respiration, ingestion, digestion, elimination. Depending on environment he might also shiver or perspire. For some reason we do not say that he circulates his blood; rather we say his blood circulates or his heart is working fine or some such thing. Yet each of the other bodily functions seems to be something that is working or happens in much the same sort of way we say that the blood is circulating. We do not think of it as something one does; it is something that goes on.

Even at this level of human existence we can distinguish two different kinds of goings on. Breathing, digestion, circulation may be distinguished from shivering and perspiring. The latter are responses to conditions in the environment: if it is hot, we perspire; if it is cold, we shiver. While the environment may influence the way we breathe or the way we circulate blood (through contraction or dilation of blood vessels), breathing and circulation *as such* are not responses to environmental stimuli.

Now, the physician might report that an infant is behaving normally with respect to the workings of these various bodily processes. Even so, we might want to say that this is not what we have in mind when we talk about human behavior. Automatic processes and automatic responses to physical stimuli are not really the doings of human beings. People do not do something called perspiring when they are put in hot environments; perspiring is something that happens under those circumstances. The physiologist may want to study the relationship of different levels and changes of climatic conditions on the perspiration and shivering mechanisms of people of various races and habitats. We would hardly want to call this the study of human *behavior* though.

Perhaps not in this sort of case; but, consider another. People perspire out of fear. They shiver in apprehension. Under emotional stress breathing may become labored or uneven. These are physiological responses, apparently automatic responses, to stimuli that do not impinge upon them in as direct a way as climate. Fear, apprehension, emotional stress are not found as such in the environment. Fear is generally of some thing. Infants are born knowing nothing. Whether fear is of physical harm or of emotional harm (as in fear of rejection) or of economic or status loss, fear is learned or acquired in some way. A physiological response to fear would interest more than the pure physiologist. It would interest the behavioral scientist as well. Some fears seem normal or healthy: an intelligent child should have enough fear of speeding automobiles to cross busy streets at properly marked walkways. Some fears are pathological: there are people with inordinate fears about leaving their homes — the very first step out of doors fills them with trembling, physical panic or nausea. We want to say that they are behaving in the most peculiar fashion. Yet, we are still talking about physiological responses to environmental phenomena. We are still talking about things that are happening to people over which they have no control.

Suppose, though, that people were to have some control over their physiological processes. The trained singer and the trained runner have learned to breathe in special ways. They quite deliberately use the lower diaphragm and they regulate intake and expulsion in accordance with the phrasing structure of the musical passage or the breathing rate they have chosen for a particular pace and distance. Some people can influence their pulse rate by sheer effort of will. Others can deliberately call to mind particular events or situations the very thoughts of which stimulate nausea, trembling, or perspiring. They can, from within, provide the environment that calls forth these responses. Indirectly, at least, they can self-nauseate, tremble or perspire.

What is it about these cases that sets them apart from the earlier ones? Processes and responses that *occur* in most people in most instances are deliberately self-manipulated by some people or in some instances. It is the character of deliberateness, of intention on the part of the agent, of agency, that leads us to call this behavior. It is something brought about by an agent that makes a process or a happening into action or behavior.

This, however, allows us to say that where there is agency, intention, deliberateness, there is action or behavior. It does not define human behavior all by itself. It may be a sufficient condition but it is not a necessary condition of behavior.

Learned Behavior

The last set of examples has already gone beyond the natural physiological repertoire of the infant. In assuming that individuals take things to be elements of the environment, in assuming purposes such as running or singing for altering physiological processes, in assuming efforts of will, we are quite a long way toward the development of the human animal into the human person. One is born a human animal; one learns to be a person. Humans have to learn to do as persons much that other animals pick up by instinct. The Lord and Master of the animal kingdom enters his Realm weaker than the lowliest of his subjects. In securing his own existence there is no creature more inept than the human infant for so long an infancy.

Learning begins early in infancy. Nor is it accidental. Whatever the family structure, there is in any society some standard set of arrangements (or in pluralistic societies some among several alternative sets) whereby the infant is to become a child and ultimately an adult. He must learn who he is, who other people are, what things are and/or what they are used for, what there is in the world and what their names are, how to chew his food, how to eat, to drink . . . So many things. He becomes a thinking, behaving person as he learns to take on the culture of the society in which he is born. As he learns the way his people identify themselves and others, as he learns their thoughts, as he learns how and what they know of the world, he learns who he is. His behavior is the behavior of his people. In what sense, then, is he an agent?

One's people provide a behavioral repertoire. In some societies behavior is much more prescribed than in others. One does not have very many alternative occupations or diversions in an isolated, technologically primitive, food gathering society. In some societies behavior is not only fairly well prescribed but there are strong proscriptions as well. Fundamentalist religious communities as, for example, the Old Order Amish prescribe a way of living and farming for their members and forbid all manner of adaptation to the modern technologically advanced pluralistic society by which they are surrounded. Their children learn what sorts of things they are to do, why they should do these things and why they should not do other things. In the primitive society, options are limited by technology and environment — one cannot choose to do what one does not know about or what is not available to do. Survival dictates much of what one does. In the Amish society one can only choose to do what one is bound by culture to do or risk expulsion. One can choose behavior in accordance with the doctrines of the group or withdrawal from the group.

Even in more modern pluralistic societies the individual's behavior is bound within limits. First of all are the obvious prescriptions and proscriptions: public laws and regulations of all sorts. One must pay one's taxes; one must not walk on the grass. 'Speed limit strictly enforced'. 'Keep to the left' or to the right or whatever. Schooling is compulsory. And so on.

Besides the list of legal Dos and Don'ts there are the 'moral' Dos and Don'ts. We are taught that there are right and wrong ways to treat other people, that there are right and wrong ways to treat ourselves or to go about our business. We generally agree across class lines and across subcultural lines that we should treat each other decently, that murder is wrong, that stealing is wrong. At least we try to get our children to believe these things even if we do not always live up to principle ourselves. And most people in most of their dealings with others do live up to principle.

There is also religious circumscription of behavior. Organized religion in one form or another tells its adherents more or less comprehensively what the limits of their freedom of action are and what their positive obligations are. Often this is coupled with ethnic or subcultural identity maintenance devices where the tie of family background and national identity and tradition place expectations and obligations on its new members. So-called modern pluralistic societies are in a sense multi-national societies.

Finally, social class, economic position and the nature of one's work all carry with them expectations about the way one lives one's life. The blue collar worker must not be 'putting on too many airs' nor can he be too different in attitudes and interests from his work mates, if he is to survive on the job in their company. The middle class executive working his way up the corporate ladder of success has to have the sort of interest and activity profile, the sort of family, and the leisure time occupation pattern that is pictured for such people as he is or wants to become. He must see himself and be seen by others as the sort who fits into the subcultural pattern defined by class, position and occupation.

One is born into a society, an ethnic group, a religion, even into a social class. One is raised to speak a particular language in a particular way. One's head is filled with ideas about right and wrong, about what people of one's sort believe or do, about occupational expectations appropriate to a child of one's background, about the proper way to bring up one's children, about the sorts of things worth doing or enjoyable to do in one's leisure time. One is usually brought up sharing experiences with members of one's sub-society. By the time one is an adult, most of one's behavior has been put on one by one's upbringing as a second skin.

Nevertheless, it is human behavior. The fact that we have been taught to say 'Hello, how are you?' when we meet does not alter the fact that we are doing that. Other people raised and living in other societies greet each other in other ways. That is the way they behave. The fact that people do the things they have been taught to do does not alter the fact of their doing them.

Each of us acquires a behavioral repertoire. In some ways it is restrictive; in any case it is permissive. It enables us to act, to do something whatever that may be. Without learning there is no human behavior. A behavioral repertoire is for all people in part, and for some virtually equivalent to, a behavioral pattern. This is the sense that I have been emphasizing, thus far. We dip into the repertoire and do the things we have been raised to do at the appropriate time and place. It is a semi-automatic response to life. It is the repertoire of the hurdy gurdy man — all punched out in order on the disc in the box. He just turns the handle.

There is another sense of repertoire, though. This is the sense in which one has a variety of things one knows how to do, a number of songs to play and ways of playing them and of combining them in the construction of different sorts of programs for different audiences and effect. If a person does not know arithmetic, he cannot become a bookkeeper. If he does know arithmetic he does not have to become a bookkeeper; he may use his knowledge of arithmetic in a variety of ways. If a person knows how to play a musical instrument, he may yet choose whether to do so. If he can ride a bike, he can ride a bike to get to work, or, if his work is delivering messages, he can ride a bike as part of work, or he can ride a bike for exercise or for pleasure or any combination of these. To have a rich variety of developed abilities is to have a range of behaviors from which to choose and in which to engage. The more liberal the society in tolerating or encouraging variety in the range of activities that people might pursue, the more behavior, though learned, may be attributed to the agency of the individual person.

The more generally applicable the abilities are that are learned in such a society the more room for agency of the individual in their particular application. It is not, by the way, that we learn general things. We learn to do specific things, but their application is general. I was taught how to count things by twos; having learned this I may count or not count by twos what I please, if I please. My counting is *my* behavior. Having been taught a language and how to write in a language, I may write what I please about whatever I wish to write. I was taught to write. Having learned to write I am able to write this book. But I was not taught nor have I learned to write this book. I am doing it. My behavioral repertoire permits me to do it. Given the difference in what I have learned about some sorts of things rather than others, it is more likely that I should write this sort of book about this sort of topic rather than some other sort about some other topic. I could not write a technical manual on the physics of sound as applied to the design and modification of stringed musical instruments. I could not very easily write a technical manual about anything. I do not know very much in the way of physics, let alone about musical instruments. Even so, I might have written about any number of subjects, and I could write a different sort of book, if I wanted to.

Much of what we do is consistent with our learned behavioral repertoire. In this sense it is not surprising that I am writing this book. It was to have been expected, though not necessarily predicted. Our behavioral repertoire is general with respect to the particulars of actual individual behavior, at least for some of us some of the time. For, we must not forget that much of what we do is not merely *consistent* with our learned behavioral repertoire; it was to have been expected *and* predicted. There are the things we are taught to do and taught to refrain from doing, performance and non-performance of which, respectively, are reinforced by social sanctions.

Let me pull some of the threads of the previous discussion together here. We can talk about individual human behavior as based in learning in three different ways. First, there is the behavioral repertoire as the behavioral pattern. The individual learns to do what is expected of him as he becomes a certain sort of person as a member of some (sub)society. Second, there is the behavioral repertoire as presenting alternatives from which the individual has learned how to do several things; he decides which of these to pursue and thereby influences or chooses what person he is or will become. Third, there is the behavioral repertoire as providing the general capabilities and skills with which the person may engage in behavior, which has not been specifically taught to him or learned by him in advance. All three sorts are genuine sorts of behavior. A student of behavior may take only one of these as the appropriate subject of inquiry. But, then, he is taking only a part of the subject. The comprehensive study of human behavior requires students of all three of these parts. It requires even more than this.

Group Behavior

Thus far I have been talking about human behavior in individual terms. Granted, learned behavior presumes a social or group context in which, or out of which, individual behavior is generated. In this important sense individual behavior is social behavior. I have raised the question of individual *vs* social agency in order to show the dividing line between the types of things that individuals may be said to do as a result of learning to be people. But now the question is raised: Are there things that groups do?

Now, I want to be careful to avoid the sort of personification of society that characterized social theorizing from early times. Society is not a person; groups are not people. There are no group minds to intend things. Individuals have hopes, fears, desires. They have minds. Groups do not have hopes, fears, desires. The people in them do, or at least some people in them do. Can a group do anything which is not the doing of its individual members?

The answer is yes and no. Individuals have to do things in order for a group to do things. But what the individuals do severally is not the same as what they do collectively. There are two basic sorts of collective behavior. There is behavior presuming a collective undertaking and there is behavior that does not but that may none the less have a collective outcome in the aggregate effect of individual and individually motivated activity.

Collectively undertaken behavior is itself readily divided into two types. First there is clearly chosen or recognized participation in a collective activity which *has* a purpose or end *for* that purpose or end. If one plays football one has to learn, understand, and adopt the rules and ends of the game. People are not just out there kicking a ball around and hurling themselves about on the grass. There are rules of play. The object is to score points, more points than are to be permitted to the other side by playing in accordance with the rules. Styles of play are dictated by consideration of the talents of the various players on each side and by consideration of tactics. Some players are primarily defensive men; others are offensive men. Certain players are designated as the ones to do the main scoring of goals. Football is engaged in by individuals as members of a team, whose activities, though different, are given meaning or point by their conscious collective endeavor.

The first type of collective behavior then is the collective endeavor, generally an organized effort to achieve some goal by rational means. At the simplest level it could consist in a couple of men coordinating their efforts to move an obstacle from their path. On a more complex level it might involve the coordination of the activities of a large number of people in a factory producing products of some sort. No one man builds the automobile; it is something they all do. If one were to look down on an automobile assembly line one would see a large number of people acting individually but in concert with one another. If one were not aware of what it was that they were doing, one might inquire about the behavior of the group on the assumption that they were not engaged in random individual behavior. One might, in similar fashion, talk about an army fighting a battle or on maneuvers or a crew operating a passenger ship.

The other sort of collective behavior undertaking involves people participating in some sort of institution but in which there is no overall direction of the activities of specific individuals. There is no product intended as in the automobile factory. There is no specific port of destination. Yet the activity is not without purpose. It may be rather unorganized and informal or it may be quite complex and formal in structure. At one end of this spectrum we might have the cocktail party; at the other end, the banking and monetary system of a modern economy.

While people may sponsor cocktail parties for all number of reasons and while people may attend them for all number of reasons, the cocktail party is a social institution that entails no specific individual outcome other than participation in a pleasurable (one would hope) social gathering. The behavior of people at a cocktail party is describable in individual behavioral terms. Individuals drink, smile, chatter, walk around, laugh, talk loudly, and the like. Doing these things and meeting some new people, renewing acquaintances, snubbing others, showing off, and the like are the sorts of behavior that one cannot engage in merely as an individual. One cannot snub someone who is not available to be snubbed. One cannot show off for someone who is not there to observe. The combination of behavior at a cocktail party is describable as cocktail party behavior. And, moreover, some people only behave in some of these ways at cocktail parties.

Group behavior, participation in the activity of the cocktail party, defines and determines individual behavior. Individual behavior may be explained and predicted by reference to cocktail party, group behavior. Similarly, the institutional setting of the productive shop, the office, the school classroom, the barracks, all provide constraints and encouragement for certain sorts of behavior of an informal socially organized sort as opposed to the structured sort rationally related to specific productive outcome. People behave differently in the classroom, teachers as well as pupils, than they do outside the classroom and that behavior is not merely a function of the business of teaching and learning specific things. That sort of purpose provides the context in which certain kinds of behavior are observed. The institutional setting of the classroom defines peer relationships differently from the playing field or the neighborhood streets. It defines peer relationships of pupils to teachers differently from those of children to parents or children to adults on the street. Teachers are held responsible for the comportment of their pupils as well as for their lessons. This places special demands on the way they deal with children. The behavior of people in institutionally defined groups is group behavior in that it is to be explained and predicted by reference to the purposes and constraints implicit in the institution.

The purpose in such a formal structured institution as a banking and monetary system is to facilitate the flow and exchange of goods and services. That is what the institution of banking and finance is for; that is what it does. We are now more or less used to the notion of a regulated system whereby some agency of government or of governments working together is responsible for trying to see to it that it achieves those purposes. Generally such systems developed without that sort of responsibility on anyone's part. In fact the institution developed along unregulated lines. Even today, while we try to hold governments or 'Wall Street' or 'the City' or the 'gnomes of Zurich' responsible for producing stability in exchange, in fact, no one is really in charge. Money is bought and sold, borrowed and loaned, risked and hedged by individuals, or commercial enterprises as well as by government agencies.

These individuals and enterprises are not interested in the purposes of the institution of finance. They are interested in their own affairs, buying, selling, borrowing, lending and the like in order to make a profit or avoid loss in the market for money or securities, or in dealing in or producing the commodities, services and products for which finance serves as a medium of exchange. Their financial behavior is defined by the system.

The system is the structural arrangements whereby people may secure and provide money or its equivalent. A person cannot pay his bills by bank cheque if his financial system does not include chequing services. Before the advent of credit cards, there was no general individual retail credit behavior to describe, explain, or predict. To explain individual financial behavior is to explain it as part of a social institution. A credit transaction is more than an individual act. It is a *transaction* or act involving a relationship at least between individuals and, in a complex financial system, among individuals as individuals, subgroups, etc. The bank card I hand to the retail clerk is linked to myriad transactions of the bank credit system together undergirding the reliability of that particular transaction. My purchase is in a sense an instance of group behavior. It is a participation in group behavior. One cannot buy a home on a mortgage loan in a society that does not permit payments of interest for use of money. The purchase of a house on a mortgage loan is not just an individual act; it is not merely a relational act of buyer and seller. It is participation in a set of mutually supporting transactions among a number of actors; it is participation in group behavior.

Group behavior by aggregation is a bit more difficult to grasp. The activities of individuals, though not coordinated by any individual or group of individuals, may yet have an effect as though they were so coordinated. That effect may have been easily predicted from the activities as an outcome or it might be a surprise, yet readily seen to flow from those activities. The effect might be desirable or undesirable, though it could hardly be called the intended outcome of the individual behavior as aggregated. Indeed, it might be the last thing the individual actors might have intended should happen. Finally, it is not something that an individual or a few individuals could have brought off by themselves.

Examples are not hard to find. Suppose the accidental coincidence of each person in a community turning on the water tap at the same moment. It is not hard to imagine that there might be such an immediate drop in water pressure for each individual tap that virtually nothing would flow through any of them. Similarly, there is the example of the 'run on the bank'. If each depositor were to appear at the same time to withdraw all his savings, there would likely be a shortage of currency with which to pay them all (as occurred during the Great Depression in a number of instances). If each pupil in a class came to school expecting to copy his assigned homework exercise from his desk mate, none of them would be able to turn in completed assignments and the teacher might be extremely cross with them all. In the first two examples each person does the same thing as the others in hopes of gaining a particular end and the joint consequence is that none of them gains that end. In the third example, each fails to do something in expectation that the others will do it. Whether failure to act and expectation are to count as behavior is at least questionable, but there is agency involved; each decided to copy, each intended to turn in the assigned work.

Now, in one sense each has participated in a group activity. One cannot turn on the tap to get water, draw money from a bank account, or fail to do home assignments unless one is a member of a society that has the appropriate institutions and one participates in them. In this sense the behavior of the individual makes sense with reference to the purposes implicit in the group activities and/or the structural environment or setting for the institution. In another sense each has participated in group behavior made possible by the setting or institution, but contrary or at least extrinsic to the purposes implicit in these. The behavior of the group in the aggregate is contrary to that which it would have been had the members of the group acted collectively.

Is it proper to call this group behavior, then? Clearly each person chooses to act in these examples. Indeed each person decides to do the same thing. While it is correct to say that the individual purposes or intentions are the same, they are common purposes only in the aggregate sense. They do not comprise some group purpose. Yet there is an effect that can only be the effect of this acting in unison, as it were. Their acting in unison does not constitute united action. The institutional arrangements make the results possible as accidents, not as implicit or defined purposes or objectives.

Consider another sort of case, the case where various people engage in behavior of different sorts, which has a result which may not have been intended by any of them. For example, suppose that passenger railroad service was operating at a loss. In the name of efficiency of operation, service is reduced along certain routes that seemed to be among the most inefficient. This has the effect of making former passengers more reliant on automobile transportation. Suppose at the same time that there has been concern over the sufficiency of supply of heating fuel for the next cold season. This concern is expressed in the demand that heating fuel production be increased relative to other productive uses of oil. Suppose further that oil companies have been experiencing increasing demand for fertilizer products and have already been shifting production in that direction. We can easily suppose a few more things, but we have enough to show the makings of an automobile fuel shortage. The aggregate of different behaviors of actors with different interests results in an unintended effect.

This seems to be stretching things, but we often do talk in this way about the behavior of the economy. There are all sorts of different decisions of different agents that go into the making and maintenance of inflation or the drop into recession. We summarize our characterization of the economy by talking about the inflationary or recessionary behavior reflected in the statistical indicators. We talk about the economy being in an inflationary spiral. We refer to certain specific behavior as inflationary in recognition of its effect on the economy given the status of other aspects of the economy. The specific behavior might not be inflationary were the state of the economy different. We characterize the behavior (say a work stoppage to obtain a wage increase in a particular industry) as inflationary even though those engaged in it do not intend inflation and even though in itself it is not inflationary. It is called inflationary because of its joint effect with continuing influences of actions taken in other sectors of the economy.

Aggregate behavior might be even more general. People have spoken of the behavior of governments, nation states, of societies, of civilizations. Spengler could write of the *Decline of the West* (1926). Marx could discuss the behavior of whole social-political-economic systems. The question is whether, at this level of generality, behavior means anything at all. The question is whether social science and the study of behavior are to be taken as synonymous. I will leave the latter question for the next chapter and the discussion of behaviorism. For now, it is worth noting: we sought to clarify what it is that we study when we study behavior in order to get at the meaning of behaviorism. It now appears that we shall have to try, as well, to clarify the meaning of behaviorism in delimiting the notion of behavior.

Still, we can make a few distinctions, now, in review. Again, we remember that we do not want to personify economy, society, or political systems. We can distinguish between structural arrangements and the behavior of people working within, influencing or being influenced by the workings of those arrangements. The study of human behavior properly includes attention to both sides of this division. But structural arrangements are not themselves behavior. The behavior of individuals in accordance with or participating in structural arrangements may be part of group behavior in either of two senses and even in both. It may be collective behavior in intent as well as effect. It may be aggregate behavior in effect, but not intent. Aggregate behavior may be all of a piece, where everyone does the same thing, or it may be varied, where people do different things. Aggregate behavior is identified as such by its effect. As we have seen, the more general the effect, the more general, or abstract even, the notion of aggregate behavior.

In asking whether this sort of generality makes the notion of behavior obscure, I want to question the business of identification by effect. Is there not a difference between accident and behavior? The fact that individuals did things intentionally does not make the joint effect of their behavior any less of an accident. A system that provides water on tap to individual households makes it possible for people acting individually to try to draw water at the same time. Everyone doing this at the same time is an accident that may or may not be planned for in the design of the water system. Were it not for the effect — no water for anyone — we would not even think of labelling the group behavior as such. The run on the bank is made possible by a financial system. Were it not for the effect — insufficient funds to pay all depositors — we would not be likely to treat a run on the bank as group behavior. The effect identifies the special event as a group event.

In this case, though, we may wonder whether such a special event is an accident. It's occurrence might be an accident. Still, it might be the result of panic in the face of rumor about the solvency of the bank. The run on the bank is then the result of the rumour. Rumour spreading may be deliberately instigated and reinforced, or it may itself be a peculiar form of group behavior. If it is deliberately instigated, then the run on the bank and the attendant insufficiency of funds have been manipulated. The event — shortage of funds — was caused deliberately. It was no accident. If the rumor just happened to be spread, again the run on the bank and the shortage were caused, but not deliberately, by the group behavior of rumor spreading. In either event the run on the bank is not group behavior in either of the collective senses, and it is still aggregate behavior. It is not in itself an accident that so many individuals demanded their money at once. Still, no one in the group need have intended the outcome — the bank's shortage of funds to meet the sudden demand.

It seems to me that we are ambivalent in our willingness to apply the term behavior to events that are accidental or unintended. On the one hand we may feel that insofar as the behavior of individuals has effects by the very fact of aggregation, they are more than mere individual acts multiplied by the numbers so acting. On the other hand, we do not want to say that people do what they do not do individually or collectively. Accidents happen to people. Effects flow from causes. The causes are not necessarily set in motion to produce their effects. We must be very careful to resist the temptation to eliminate our ambivalence by attributing agency or intention to aggregate group behavior and seeking always the god or the devil in the social machinery. 'Someone or something is responsible for the bank's running short of funds.' Often the agent responsible is the 'system' and then we are involved in personification, mysticism, or both.

Perhaps there is a fundamental commitment to the idea of agency in our notion of behavior, or at least of human behavior, that is hard to ignore. Whether we are talking abut individuals or groups we want to be able to distinguish what happened from what was done. The question is not merely, 'Did he fall or was he pushed?' The question is 'Did he fall, was he pushed, or did he jump?' The question is 'Did they fall, were they pushed, or did they jump?' It is time to take another look at behavior focusing more carefully on agency and the responsibility for behavior.

Human Behavior and Responsibility

Earlier, I spoke of the individual learning to become a person in a society by taking on the behavioral repertoire made available to him through learning. Three senses of acting in accordance with a behavioral repertoire were discussed in an exploration of the notion of agency. In one sense, the individual appeared to be more a creature of his upbringing than an agent; he seemed to be an automaton rather than a person. The other senses of behavioral repertoire left increasingly more room for the person as agent. Indeed, the sense in which the person had a repertoire of capabilities to be exercised as he decided emphasized the responsibility of the agent for his behavior. The individual is given credit for what he does; he is the conductor and orchestrator of his own activities. He is also held accountable for what he does for just these very reasons. His behavior is not blind mimicking of social ritual. He is not repeating the history of his race as its instrument in the present generation. His behavior is his because he has chosen it and adapted his repertoire, his cultural legacy, to his own ends.

But now, we might ask, where do these ends come from? We might easily respond with an analysis of responsible behavior in terms of repertoire of ends. Thus we might point to particular sorts of things one might try to achieve as selected by one's society or subculture. As in the earlier analysis the ends may be incorporated in the behavior. If one wants to be a full-fledged accepted member of one's class or caste one will try to emulate the behavior of such members or aspirants as achieve success. We are more interested in the person who chooses the purposes toward which he will select and apply his generalizable capabilities. We have characterized the society that makes this possible as more liberal with regard to the sorts of things one might do.

In a sense this is tantamount to saying that the society is more liberal with regard to the purposes or ends that individuals might pursue. There are some general sorts of human ends. People may seek comfort, security, companionship, fame, respect, riches, satisfaction of all sorts of appetites and the like. These may be emphasized or available to greater or lesser degree in different societies. The means to their attainment may be more or less varied in different societies. In one society, the routes to ends are narrowly circumscribed; much comes to him who does adopt the behavioral pattern of the group as it comes to him. In other societies there are a variety of things one can do in order to achieve 'success' and in monetary economies success may be financial with attendant opportunity for conversion of financial success into the achievement of a number of those more general personal ends.

There may be greater choice in the types of activities that one may engage in than in those ultimate sorts of ends. One may wish prominence as a musician, or as a merchant or as an athlete. The activity becomes a part of the end. The means and end are intertwined. Behavior is not merely directed toward an end; it is undertaken in part, or in a sense, for its own sake. Granted, one may choose among ends such as monetary reward or the respect (self or from others) that comes from mastery of craft or instrument, or from service to others. Still, for most of us the choice is not merely a choice of ends, it is a choice of how we will live our lives, a choice of a way of life, or what we will do, of the sorts of behavior we are likely to engage in. And for most of us, I would guess, it is initially, at least, not recognized as such. We probably do not know what we are letting ourselves in for, as we choose our ends and occupations. This is especially true if we do not blindly follow in the way of life in which we have been raised. The more choice we have, the more opportunity there is to choose that for which experience has scarcely prepared us.

What sense, then, can be made of the notion of responsibility for our choices. If the choices are ours, they are ours. No one else has made them. I suppose we are responsible for them. But if we do not know what our choices entail until we have made them, how can we choose responsibly; how can we be held accountable for the act of choice?

There is an equivocation here in the meaning of responsibility and of accountability. On the one hand, we mean merely that the individual made the choice. He was not coerced. It was not made for him. Since it is his, freely chosen, no one else can be blamed for it or given credit for it. On the other hand we mean that he is responsible for knowing what he has chosen. He has chosen responsibly, in consideration of the implications of his choice in his future behavior or obligations especially as they impinge on the legitimate expectations of others. He may be held accountable for his obligations to future behavior for himself or to others thereby incurred.

We cannot legitimately legislate in favor of one sense over the other here, when we are talking about responsible behavior. We cannot require prescience, or wisdom beyond one's years as a condition of indicating that behavior was freely chosen by an agent, that he did it. At the same time, we may want to set down as a condition of agency of free choice that the individual should have given some consideration to what he was letting himself in for, that even if his judgment about this was mistaken his choice was no mere accident. He did not just fall into it. Or, perhaps more accurately, even if the choice was accidental or the agent just fell into it, we want him to *take responsibility* for his behavior, for the duties or obligations following upon his choice. This last point will need a bit of explanation.

How can one's choice be a matter of chance or something that one has fallen into? Well, most simply, given a range of options one way of deciding among them is to spin the wheel and take what comes up. Or, given a range of options in occupations and ends that one might pursue, one is offered the opportunity to pursue one of them 'out of the blue' and takes it. One chooses by letting it happen. To let the wheel do it for one is to choose whatever comes up, even if one needs to choose something. If one is not desperate, one need not choose the first opportunity that presents itself. One can be held responsible as agent for choosing by letting it happen, so long as one could have chosen otherwise. Or, can one?

There is a view that would deny the meaning of choice and responsibility altogether. On this view all individual behavior is a matter of letting it happen. All group or large scale behavior, if the scale is large enough, is also a matter of letting it happen. Collective behavior of the productive or end-directed sort is glossed over. Let us examine this view beginning with the individual.

The freedom of the individual and the determinism of behavior are somehow supposed to be incompatible. If behavior is determined in the scientific sense, it is not a matter of random accident. It has antecedents by which it is explained or predicted. If, as we noted in the last chapter, knowledge of human behavior is to be placed on the same plane as knowledge of animal behavior, then humans are to be free to choose in the same way that animals are free to choose. One explains and predicts choices as items of behavior. Humans may decide to do something and subsequently do it, perhaps even do it a long time after the decision. Perhaps animals do not. Perhaps animal choice and action constitute one behavior. At any rate we are aware of the possibility of time delay between human deliberation and choice and subsequent expression of that choice in action. Accordingly, we treat deliberation and choice as behavior separate from the subsequent action. We try to account for the individual's choice. We may try to do so in a way that makes the idea of choice eliminable.

To explain or predict an event by reference to its antecedents one must have some laws, or rules of thumb at least, about the relationship of antecedents of that sort to events of the appropriate sort. For reasons that I shall not go into right now, having to do with types of laws and relationships, it is rather easy to suppose (incorrectly) that if certain events occur they must be followed by certain other events, or if certain events occurred they must have been preceded by certain other events. Things do not just happen in the world of nature: they proceed from causes; they proceed to effects. Human choices do not just happen: they proceed from causes; they proceed to effects. If one knows the causes of specific human choices, then one can project the choice and the effects of that choice. The cause of the choice is the cause of the ultimate behavior. Choice is eliminable on that view, or it is kept around as a mediating step between 'real' causes and the ensuing behavior. In either case, by treating choice itself as a behavior to be explained, it is explained away.

If choice is explained away, the individual is an agent only in the sense of one who carries out the dictates of someone or something else. Literally, he cannot carry out the dictates of someone else unless we can find someone else responsible for these dictates. That is, all individuals in a chain of command, as it were, are agents carrying out the dictates of the next one up the chain. Each, then, can be said to have no dictates of his own to pass on. Ultimately, someone or something has to be at the top. It cannot be an individual someone, if we insist that each instance of agency involves carrying out dictates arising external to the agent. There is an infinite regression here.

One may try, as the neo-Freudians do, to put the 'external' source of choice and behavior back inside the individual. It is not always clear whether the individual personality is comprised of pseudo-persons contending with one another (a throwback to Plato's personification of the parts of the soul where the appetites were at war with one another, where reason sought command of the courageous and strong element to control appetites for the sake of harmony), or whether the environment and experience of the individual are taken inside in such a way that one's past is always available as cause of present behavior. If the latter seems more plausible, it is because, first we do recognize the influences of past experiences on present behavior. After all, what we know or believe and feel is what we have learned on our way to the here and now. Second, it is because we explain behavior in nature in terms of experience and the influence of the environment. We observe creatures responding to stimuli as presented to them. We see them respond to stimuli on the basis of their past experience with them. It is only a small step, but a large leap, to the conclusion that all behavior is a matter of response to previously stored stimuli, remembered or otherwise.

The mechanisms for such storing of stimuli are the attitudes, dispositions, or propensities that we are said to have. And, indeed, we do admit to having characteristic responses to various sorts of situations or events. People tend to be cautious, or daring, in the face of new experiences. People may tend to seek such experiences. Given the chance, some people will do some things rather than other things. We do many things as a matter of course; we engage in many activities as a matter of habit. The social drinker is disposed to drink when the occasion presents itself. The habitual drinker has a propensity to drink; he creates his own occasion for drinking. Perhaps more strongly, he cannot help himself in so doing. He is not merely disposed; he is driven.

It would be foolish to deny that there are people so 'driven' that they engage in behavior as though compelled against their will. Indeed, we talk of the compulsive drinker, and the compulsive worker, the compulsively punctual. It is foolish to deny that a good bit of human behavior is habitual or programmed in the course of growing up. What is more foolish or misguided is to construe *all* behavior as driven or compelled by someone or something in the individual.

There are two main reasons why this is so. First, the behavioral repertoire available to us from which we might choose what to do is ambiguous with respect to the attitudes, dispositions and (non-pathological) propensities we carry around with us. The very same attitudes may be expressed in a variety of activities. One likes people — that does not entail that one should be a public servant, that one should be a doctor, lawyer or carpenter or plumber. One likes to take risks — but as an entrepreneur or a parachutist? One is curious — but as a classicist, a chemist, or weekend explorer? The choices, as I pointed out earlier, are consistent with the behavioral repertoire of a given individual and his recognition or knowledge of the opportunities, but they are not *compelled* by the individual's knowledge and experience to be what they are. They happen to be what they are because the individual has chosen them.

Second, in an economically developed, culturally complex society the experience of the individual does not present limited stimuli and uniform reinforcement of very specific behaviors to the exclusion of alternatives. Rather, stimuli conflict; reinforcements conflict. The individual is subject to all sorts of pushes and pulls from family, from friends, and chance acquaintances, on the street, in school, on the job, on the playground, in church. Many of these influences are at cross purposes to one another; some have greater impact than others. Most are uncontrolled by any specific agency. Somehow, they all impinge upon the individual and it is only through his behavior, it is only through his choices as applied, that we infer their organization in a given direction. There is no way we can know independently what the balance of his past experiences have been such that they influence his choice one way rather than another. Knowing something about his background, we may be able to predict what sorts of things he is likely to do rather than what other sorts of things. Still, we cannot say that his background compelled him to do these things, just because we are willing to state the odds on his doing them. If his background is composed of relatively uniform stimuli and reinforcement of certain choices from a limited behavioral repertoire and limited range of perceived options, then we might at least say that his choice was narrowly constrained. Nevertheless, we cannot show that it was compelled. In those cases where the repertoire is expansive, opportunities abound and are perceived so, experience has been broad ranging in number and variety of contacts with individuals and activities — in such cases it is impossible to assess the impact of 'forces' that make the individual choose as he does, do as he does. To say that his behavior represents the balance of the forces acting on him is gratuitous. It says nothing except by mere assertion that a man chooses what he chooses because he has to so choose.

Stop and think about a choice you have to make. Does it make any difference to you that your choice is what it is ordained to be somehow by your past? Do you feel your choice made for you? Is it made any easier on this assumption? Of course not! You still have to choose. Whatever you choose must necessarily be consistent with what you were ordained to choose by your past. It appears that we cannot know that we do not have freedom of choice as agents for our behavior, and that we are constrained to act as though we do have such choice, at least some of the time. Accordingly, the attempt to characterize all human behavior as in some sense compelled is doomed to frustration.

To characterize it as somehow compelled by forces acting in the individual is to engage in mysticism. It is to invent fictional entities to account for what we cannot know. There is another sort of compulsion by forces that challenges the notion of individual choice — forces acting outside the individual. On this view, freedom of the individual through choice is the myth.

The individual's freedom is constrained by social forces; the individual only thinks that he is choosing freely. It is not some mechanism inside the individual that chooses for him, but mechanisms beyond his control in society, or history or the economy. The individual, on this account, is acting out his part in some sort of grand design. History has decreed that certain events shall be followed by other events. The laws of society once set in motion by events move men inevitably from era to era of social development or through the evolution of the stages of social organization. What is not clear here are the mechanisms by which the individual is moved as the cog in the societal evolutionary machine.

What is not clear here are the means by which forces move people and events. What is wanted is something more than a detailing of the means by which individuals are socialized into participation in ongoing institutions and patterns of living. We do not have to invent forces of some sort to account for that — that is the ongoing business of the various social sciences. What we need is an account showing why it is that the choices individuals make, whether to act privately or in concert, are somehow necessarily the choices they have to make. More than that, we need an account of how individuals are *made* to make those choices.

To say that people are forced to make the choices that they do make is to say nothing. People do make the choices they make. They could have done otherwise or these would not be choices. That they have at any time chosen what they have chosen tells us nothing about constraint. We might ask rhetorically, 'Given the kinds of people they are, given their experience, given their situation, how could they have chosen otherwise?' But this is only a rhetorical question. However well we might predict what the decision is likely to be, unless we have the social laws relating specifiable characteristics of these people, of their experience, of their situation to predict such behavior in advance, we have only hindsight to tell us that there were forces making them so choose. Forces becomes the name for those laws relating specifics, laws of which we are ignorant, if we must so name them.

One might look back through time to great movements in the affairs of men, movements which had a profound effect upon the course of history. The spread of the Roman Empire gave a cultural unity to the western world that underlies western thought and culture to this day. The industrial revolution is still working itself out, whether to fruition or perdition is not yet clear. And in the time between those movements there took place the development and spread of organized religion, feudalism, the rise of mercantile capitalism, great crusades, intercontinental wars of east and west, and so many other events or occurrences each overshadowing the individual lives of the people living through and in them. Here are events spanning centuries, covering vast areas of the world. The individual person in his individual spot on earth seems as a speck of dust. In the aggregate, we seem as the very earth itself, moved and shaped by the grand sweep of history.

If only we could know the forces at work in history, we could understand where we have come from and where we are going. Had Newton not raised his view from the dust of ordinary physical experience, he would not have discovered the sweeping universal laws explaining behavior in and of the physical world. The social scientist of the more ambitious sort seeks to explain the course of human behavior in social laws of an analogous sort. The difference is, of course, that Newton's invisible forces acting at a distance could be shown and illustrated through precise calculation as acting on particular items in physical nature. The overambitious social scientist would explain human behavior by social forces that cannot be shown by anything like this to be acting on specific items of human behavior and especially human choice.

Lage scale human behavior, behavior over vast times and places, cannot be simplified in this way. Looked at over time, over its development, it may seem to have a unity, it may appear as a whole. We speak of *its development*. And yet *it* is not the behavior of any individual. *It* may not be the behavior of any group of individuals, at least not in the collective sense. Perhaps *it* is the aggregate social behavior but in a special sense. It is the aggregation of the interplay of the behavior of individuals, of collective groups, of aggregates over time as they influence and are influenced by one another and by their natural and social environments. In this sense large scale human behavior is a mixture of the variety of human choices, behavior, enterprises, perceptions as well as the accidents of nature that impinge upon their activities for good or ill. In this sense, no *one* or *ones* are responsible for large scale human behavior.

This does not make large scale behavior mysterious in some sense. It does not mean that one cannot identify the responsibility for elements of its development in individual choice and behavior at particular times and places. It does not mean that one cannot trace the path of development over time in the activities of particular people in response to particular environmental situations both social and natural. It means, on the contrary, that one may only explain large scale behavior through the effort to trace out the course of specifically human behavior through laws and generalizations about human behavior. Social science must be behavioral science if it is to be science at all. Whether one must be a behaviorist to do behavioral science is another question.

CHAPTER 3

Behaviorism

In the discussion of human behavior it was useful, indeed it seemed necessary, to introduce considerations relating to the scientific study of behavior. The scientific study of behavior requires a view of its subject matter as amenable to observation, measurement, control, precise identification and description. The methods of scientific categorization in the natural sciences should be applicable in the behavioral sciences. The natural scientist studying the phenomenon of combustion needed to eliminate the non-specifiable, non-observable, non-identifiable, non-describable *phlogiston*. This was the substance or entity supposedly accounting for the occurrence of combustion. This was replaced by an account of combustion that relied on more precise identification of the elements in the process, their relationships as specified by controlled observation and chemical analysis of the effects of their absence and presence under specifiable conditions. Combustion had to be defined in such a way as to be available for scientific study. The value of the definition is established in the success of the scientific study to make specific the working of what was previously a gross process. By analogy the success of any account of human behavior will be evaluated in the character of the specification provided by behavioral science.

In the last chapter behavior was not so much defined as it was delimited. We have only gone so far as to discuss what is to count as human behavior. It remains for behavioral science to explain how it works — to define it in its workings.

Now, just as the natural sciences are not all of a piece — physics is a quite different sort of science from zoology, for example — the behavioral sciences constitute a rather mixed bag, as well. Natural scientists, or their fellow travellers, tend to forget this as they characterize the 'hard' sciences as though they had the 'hardness' of physics. So too, behavioral scientists might try to define themselves by the example of behavioral psychology. This will lead us to the question later on of 'reductionism'. For now though, I would rather focus attention on the notion of studying behavior. What makes behavioral sciences behavioral? What makes them scientific?

The Behavioral Sciences

Most institutions of higher education in the United States divide their curricular offerings and academic departments in the arts and sciences into three broad divisions, the humanities, the natural sciences, and the social sciences. The social sciences are generally held to include the subjects of economics, government (or political science), sociology, anthropology and history. Sometimes psychology, especially social psychology, is included under the social sciences. Often, though, psychology is placed in the natural science division. Yet psychology is usually the first subject to come to mind as a behavioral science. History is the last of these to be so labeled. In fact, there has always been some debate whether it should be labeled a social science at all, or whether America should follow the English usage and put it in with the humanities. Some ways of doing political science or sociology lead one to raise similar questions about these fields. Economics often seems more a branch of mathematics (which in the United States is lumped into the natural sciences) than a social science.

If the social sciences need sorting out, it should be clear as well that they are not synonymous with the behavioral sciences in some direct or simple way. Yet it is not clear just how to draw the line. We might want to eliminate the discipline of history on grounds that much of its practice is hardly scientific on anything like the natural science model. But history, of all the disciplines, has provided us with the most comprehensive account or record of human behavior, individual, social, institutional, international — all kinds. What about specialties in biology — anatomy, physiology, kinesiology — as they deal with human behavior? Should these be included in the behavioral sciences, even though they are not generally thought of as social sciences? They certainly tell us a great deal about human behavior (or at least about the mechanisms of it) and go about their business as *bona fide* Natural Sciences. Now, we do not want to say that any (sub)discipline whose study is human behavior, or strongly bears on that topic, should count as a behavioral science. For then we would spread the net too widely — widely enough to include philosophy with its sub-fields of ethics or philosophy of mind and indeed just about all its branches. It would include physics and chemistry. After all, we are subject to the laws of motion and mechanics; we are made up of all sorts of chemical compounds; human thinking and action proceed through electro-chemical mechanisms. Everything cannot count as a behavioral science for then the notion of behavioral science would be hopelessly ambiguous; it would not serve to distinguish among the disciplines. This would not do.

The criterion for inclusion was too broad. For a discipline to count as a behavioral science it should study human behavior *as* human behavior. This would eliminate the general fields of physics or chemistry or biology as these are concerned with advancing knowledge of physical, chemical or biological phenomena *per se.* They may contribute to an understanding of human behavior as they are applied by students of human behavior toward that end. Some of the practitioners of the natural scientific disciplines may be interested in direct contribution to the understanding of human behavior — for example, the basis in chemical balance of various human organs of dispositions toward irascibility or aggressive behavior. In such cases the practitioner may indeed be called a behavioral scientist. His research may become a hybrid sub-speciality, a behavioral science.

The new criterion may be too narrow, though. Behavioral psychology with its emphasis on laboratory experimentation might also be eliminated. While the object is to find general laws of behavior, to place man in the animal kingdom, much if not most of the experimental work is with animals other than man. Animal experimentation may be viewed as the behavioral scientist's equivalent to the early physicist's fiddling around with inclined planes and creating vacuums to simulate action of objects in space. This is a simplification of nature in order to observe and measure its workings purely and simply. So too, experimental psychologists are, or profess to be, concerned to understand human behavior purely and simply through their work with animals free of all interfering cultural impediments. But this is not studying human behavior. It is not studying human behavior *as* human behavior.

Now it is not my business to define the behavioral sciences. If they seem to be comprised of the loose bag I spoke of earlier, of social science and behavioral psychology, then so be it. If we are prepared to enlarge our conception to include other fields insofar as they are directly concerned to advance understanding of human behavior as human behavior, all well and good. Perhaps there is no single criterion by which to identify a behavioral science. Perhaps, though, there are characteristics that mark off behavioral as against non-behavioral approaches within the relevant disciplines.

I say approaches here quite deliberately. I want to emphasize methodology. If we have the common sense, but fuzzy, idea that behavioral sciences are about behavior, we have, as well, an equally fuzzy idea that they ought to be scientific in the way they go about it. The quest continues for that science of human behavior I spoke of earlier. But, with the development of the several academic disciplines we seem to have several sciences of human behavior. Whether these may yet be a unified science of behavior remains to be seen. Still, there is a theme uniting the behavioral approach across the various disciplinary lines.

There is a commitment to scientific methodology. Recalling that with the natural sciences there are broad differences in scientific practice, we should be alert to differences here as well. There is no single road to scientific truth, about man in society or man in nature. Nevertheless, there is what might be called a general scientific outlook, the concern for the systematic construction of knowledge.

At bottom, there is the business of gathering data in a systematic fashion. What 'everyone knows' or what the 'old China hand knows' or what 'anyone who has ever been there knows' is replaced by information available to those who have not been there. Common sense is, in practice, often indistinguishable from common nonsense. Armchair social science often substitutes what one thinks ought to be the case for what in fact is the case.

Now, this might seem fairly obvious, but a good bit of modern social science began with the simple effort to count things, to amass information in detail. We talk rather easily now about *per capita* income, or disposable income, or balance of payments and trade deficits, but someone had to develop systematic procedures for counting people and calculating national income, and for keeping track of the flow of money and goods in international trade. Is the economy looking up? How would one decide? To begin with, one must have information on which to base a decision.

Information does not present itself for enumeration and classification. One must decide what sorts of information one wants. Classification and information gathering are two sides of a coin. Anthropology has its roots in the accounts of explorers and merchants who returned home from their travels with wondrous tales of the strange lands and peoples and customs they had seen. At times these tales were more fiction than fact. Factual accuracy could be improved to the extent that the travelers kept journals and recorded their observations on the way. Anthropology took a step forward as individuals made it their business to travel and live among various peoples for long periods of time for the very purpose of recording their observations about them. Anthropology assumed some sort of scientific status when such observation was made systematic through the adoption of a set of categories. Anthropologists could agree on the institutions of culture that appeared to be universal (governance, family structure and kinship, religion, food preparation, etc.). They could then impress upon those who would study in the field the importance of observing and recording information pertaining to these institutions. In this way description could be made both comprehensive and comprehensible. Moreover, it would permit comparison of cultures and it would permit the study of the generality or universality of particular social practices or combinations of practices and beliefs. One could observe human behavior as human behavior, directly in the field, living with the members of a given society under study, asking them questions, participating in their activities and systematically making and recording one's observations in a format readily intelligible to other anthropologists. Recorded observations could be coded and filed for easy cross-reference access. The whole thing could be stored in computers in manipulable form and all manner of sorting and statistical evaluation would be possible. And, indeed, this has happened.[1]

This is, at bottom, the same sort of approach one finds in sociology and political science. There may be differences in the manner in which data is gathered, depending upon the research interests of particular investigators. Some research is very much like ethnography — observing behavior, recording expressed attitudes, asking questions in working class bars (pubs) or in school classrooms or staffrooms. Other research involves more 'intervention', as in experimental variation in the environment of the work place by comparison with the 'control' — unchanged work place for similarly engaged workers. There may be greater reliance on specialized techniques of asking questions — survey research instruments, questionnaires, tests or exams — as against long-term observation and questioning. This limited span of observation time places a greater burden on the construction of questions and the analysis of response or response patterns for such instruments. In turn, this gives rise to a tendency to confuse research methodology in sociology or political science with the methodology of statistical evaluation. At the extreme, the substance of behavioral science is subverted at the expense of fiddling around with mathematical analysis of data. The quality of the data may not be worthy of any such analysis.[2]

At any rate, as sociology and political science rely increasingly on survey and questionnaire instruments they move one step away from the direct observation of human behavior as human behavior: they ask people to describe what they have done, what they are doing, what they would do 'if . . .'. They ask for attitudes, reasons, beliefs, knowledge. They may seek to dig into some specific behavioral phenomenon, as in explaining the results of a particular election or the tendency of immigrants from certain national backgrounds to settle into particular occupations rather than others. Still, the emphasis is now on the creation of data in a scientific way for analysis in scientific ways. The data must still be categorized, only now new categories and entities may suggest themselves as hybrids developing out of such instrumentation and analysis. Several questions may be answered consistently in one pattern by some individuals and in another pattern by other individuals. One might then focus on the differences in the two groups of individuals and thereby name them as groups. One might also focus on the difference in patterns of response naming these as entities, even as theoretic entities.[3]

When it comes to sophistication in use of mathematical technique and in the development thereby of theoretic entities and structures, economics appears to be the queen of the social sciences. In other fields it is often harder to interpret data. Attitudes, beliefs, opinions, intentions are not easy to evaluate, to weigh numerically, to compare. While there is certainly room for sophisticated discussion of alternative measuring devices, economics as a field does benefit from the relative ease of quantification of data developed over centuries of mercantile and industrial practice. Numbers of people are numbers of people. Quantities of goods, units of production are provided in established business practices. Goods and services are evaluated in dollars, or pounds sterling, or yen, or marks. The economist may ask questions of businessmen or ordinary consumers in the same way as the sociologist. More typically he takes his data from the record of their activities as reflected in census reports of one kind or another, in reports of supplies of goods or of money, of new construction, of capital, or housing starts, or government purchase of goods and services. The economist tends to be hard headed. Better to gauge the intentions of a producer by his actions than his words. Are his sales down and inventories up, is he hiring or laying off workers, bidding for materials, investing in new plant and equipment? Things take time; tomorrow's events must be set in motion today and today is a matter of record.

It is the record of behavior rather than the behavior itself that constitutes the economist's data. In this sense he does not observe human behavior as human behavior; he observes the record of human behavior in order to account for other behavior and to predict future behavior. His language is often behavioral and attitudinal as he talks about 'propensities to save or consume', or 'indicators of business confidence' and the like. But this language is a behavioral gloss on the record of savings over spending for consumption, or savings as against investment.

His main interest is to be able to describe the state of the economy (or some segment of it) in such a way that he can project other states of the economy (or segment) at other times. He may be concerned at the level of the firm or industry — say as an industrial analyst or business adviser. He may be concerned more generally in national economic policy planning. In either case he needs some way of relating several variables such that he can evaluate the impact of changes in the values of some of them on the others.

He seeks not merely systematic observation, classification and manipulation of his data; he seeks system *in* his data. Now, other social scientists seek system as well — they talk about social systems, kinship systems, political systems, etc. The economist has been working at systems expressible in mathematical equations. He wants to describe the economic system in terms of process laws much as physics seeks to describe the natural world. The economist seeks the social equivalent of nature's $E = mc^2$, the identification of invariant relationships among theoretic entities that serve in their general character to illuminate and help to specify all manner of additional particular relationships. He seeks the social equivalent of the speed of light, a constant value, a solid rock in a sea of shifting variables, an anchor by which they may be tied together in a structure or network.

To seek is not yet to find. Economics is the most theoretico-mathematical of the social sciences. It has sought to identify, or perhaps better to invent, certain social constants. But they are not yet fixed or certain. Economics makes greater use of the calculus and higher forms of mathematics than any of the other behavioral sciences in an effort to find these constants and/or work around them. Its basic data is behavior as recorded. Its aim is to discover the processes by which the record changes. It is most self-consciously aimed at becoming the social physics envisioned two centuries earlier. As such, it seems far removed from the study of human behavior. And it is not clear how the social physics of an economics will inform our understanding of human behavior as it is viewed by the other behavioral sciences. Perhaps an economic determinist might take such a position, but it is hard to see just how economics bears the same relationship to the general human behavior that physics bears to the other natural sciences.

Now, I mentioned earlier that the natural sciences are not all of a piece. Granted that physics underlies an understanding of all of physical nature — nature is physical. Granted that there is a considerable theoretic overlap of physics and chemistry say, such that much of chemistry is expressible in more fundamental terms of physics. Nevertheless, much of what chemists do and much of what interests them are rather different from what physicists do and are interested in. The geologist may use some physics and/or chemistry in his work, but his primary interest may be to explain the history of the movement of the earth's crust, for example, and his methods may involve a good bit of digging, classifying, comparing, etc. The biologist or zoologist hardly needs much physics to go about his work. This work does, nonetheless, inform our knowledge of nature. It is scientific as much as physics is scientific. All of science cannot be reduced to physics.

All of behavioral or social science cannot be reduced to economics. There may be economic motivations in the way we vote or in the way family institutions are developed. There may be economic interpretations of the rise and fall of the influence of organized religion. But, one can study social phenomena in a variety of ways with a variety of interests without being very much informed by proto-process laws of economics. Moreover, there is no reason to suppose that laws about the 'behavior of the economy' or of 'economic behavior' are somehow definitive of the 'behavior of society' or of human behavior in general. However general it is in its theoretic approach, economics is the study of one among a number of categories of social life. Economic behavior is behavior within a particular socially defined institutional framework. Indeed, one might wonder whether there is some more general science of behavior to inform the behavioral sciences, including economics.

The Science of Behavior

Perhaps psychology with its roots in the biological sciences and medicine might serve as the source of the general laws of behavior. Of course psychology is itself hardly a unified discipline. It is more like a congeries of fields, which may yet be aggregated under three main headings, though there is some intermingling here and there. The headings are physical, mental, and behavioral. I wish I could think of a better name for the third category so that it would not sound like the candidate of choice for the science of behavior. But, after all, it does reflect usage and it is promoted as just such a candidate. Still, the aim under all these headings is to understand behavior, so there is some observation of behavior implicit in all of them.

The physical approach in psychology represents an emphasis on the physical mechanisms of behavior. Perhaps the most general category here is physiological psychology. Even this covers a broad range of investigative activity. It includes everything from experimentation on stimulus reception — visual, tactile, taste, etc. with humans or roaches or any of the other orders in between. It includes everything from observation of behavior to the monitoring of electrical or chemical changes of the organism in response to stimulus. Stimuli may be presented to the natural organs of sense, or presented more directly to the brain or nervous system through electrical impulse along a series of probes. It includes everything from classical conditioning of physiological responses to stimuli *à la* Pavlov's dog, to neurosurgery.

The stress here is not so much on the conditioning of behavior as it is on the tracing of the pathways through the human animal from stimulus to response. This, by the way, is *my* stress as I am defining the heading. There are many people doing experimental work who are only interested in determining stimulus thresholds — for example the levels of intensity, or modes of presentation at which or by which stimuli are perceived or not perceived. Such people may not care at all about the internal mechanisms of perception. Others may be more interested in locating those areas of the brain that control the processing of stimuli from the different organs of perception. Yet others may be interested in the relaying of messages through the central nervous system from perception to the brain and thence again to activate the physical response of the organism. The heading, or category, 'physical psychology' is intended to include the elements of the whole investigative process whether or not the individual investigators included are dealing with the process inclusively.

The sense in which this sort of business contributes to an understanding of behavior is much like the sense in which understanding what each item in a kit of carpenter's tools can be used for as applied to wood explains how particular workmen operate. One can do more with a full kit of tools than with a small one. Surely, we might identify some differences in behavior as due to differences in individual capacity to behave in certain ways. A color blind person does not respond to the same stimuli as a normal person in the same ways. He does not see the same stimuli as stimuli. Dogs respond to smells and sounds of which humans are totally unaware. People have large complex brain and neurological structures permitting them to use language to remember and manipulate all sorts of information, which can eventuate in the sort of behavior that is not available to other species. It is possible to stimulate overt behavior through fiddling with probes in someone's brain. But this is on a rather gross level of inducing reaction to perception of what isn't really out there. Physical psychology is not the study of human behavior as human behavior; it is more the study of the physical limits and possibilities implicit in the human machine. It is the continuation of La Mettrie's quest (1748). It is the study of human behavior as animal behavior and it is thereby limited.

Mental psychology would overcome this limitation by emphasizing that man is more than a machine. Man has a mind as well as a brain. Human behavior is not mere animal behavior. That highly developed brain and neural structures making possible the storing and manipulation of complex information make mind possible. The brain stores; the mind thinks, believes, fears, judges. These are more than physical; they are mental. The capacity of the machine to accommodate the demands and rise to the richness of the possibilities of language and culture, of sense to accommodate sensibility, is only an index to the workings of mind in behavior. One must study the workings of mind in behavior more directly.

Now, how is this to be done? By definition, the mind is not physical. If the physical system is only an indirect entré into mind what is there to observe directly as mind? Well, if mind is thinking, believing, judging, feeling, fearing, and the like, we might ask people to open their minds (or their mouths) to observation. We might ask them to make explicit what is going on in their heads as they do something. We might try to get them to put into words what went on in their heads when they did something in the past. We might try to make sense out of their behavior by grounding it in a reconstruction of the mix of beliefs, attitudes and emotions influencing that behavior — a sort of reconstruction of the state of mind, as it were. We might make sense of their behavior as making good sense, as reasonable if one knows the reasons.

There are difficulties with these various sorts of observation. Chief among these difficulties is that of sorting out the inferences of the reporting subject and of the investigator in getting at the sources or meaning of the subject's behavior. Still, one can overstate this problem. Let us begin with the most straightforward case.

There has long been an interest in understanding the nature of intelligent behavior. We know that solving a problem, say in geometry doing a proof, is not merely a matter of presenting the solution. We know that some people seem to be good at presenting solutions and others are not. We do not want to know here how the problem is solved, that is we do not want the solution. We want to know how individuals go about arriving at solutions. Do they use particular techniques, are there special steps that successful solvers follow in applying these techniques, do people use the same sorts of algorithms that might be programmed for computer solution to like problems or do people solve problems differently?[4]

One way to get at these questions is to ask people to 'think out loud' as they work at solutions to problems. In that way one might record what goes into successive stages of preparing the solution. Is there immediate recognition of the problem as being of a certain type, reduction of a new problem to elements that are more familiar, random trying out of different approaches, or random trying of different axioms or postulates? Do some people see problems spatially as well as logically and is there imaginative manipulation of space through visual reconception of the problem through analysis into sub-figures or structures or construction as part of a new whole? Do some people seem to know when this is promising as a solution strategy and others not? Do some people hypothesize conclusions to open-ended problems and work from 'both ends' of the problem to the middle filling out the solution in between?

At times the solutions to the problems themselves allow inference to these sorts of things, but they do not tell how the person got to the given solution. The solution does not contain all the false starts, blind alleys, and choices made and rejected along the way. The idea is to have the problem solver tell us these things as he goes along. The difficulty is that the problem solver may not himself be able to tell us how he solves a problem. He may have some general idea of things he might do as he approaches a problem, but he might not know how, or why, promising leads come to his head. One must have certain information and understanding to apply to the solution of a problem, but how is it that some of us are most efficient in mining that information and utilizing the understanding while others are not? How is it that some of us see a problem as best handled by manipulation or reconstruction while others do not? And we cannot catch ourselves at doing any kind of thinking that we can describe in words while we are doing it other than that we are doing it. Perhaps intelligent behavior *may not* be analyzable into two things — intelligence and behavior — in such a way that their relationship might be examined. Then again, we can at times make explicit some of the things we do when we do things intelligently.[5]

I suspect, though, that this is a sort of inference that we draw from our own behavior rather than a direct awareness of the immediate process of behavior. Solving a problem, to continue the example, does not usually involve a conscious effort to figure out how to solve the problem. We do not usually take ourselves to be solving two problems: the problem as given to us and the problem of how to solve the problem as given to us. (Then, I suppose one might wonder how to solve the problem of how to solve the problem, etc., etc.) In fact, one might say, 'Hmm, how am I going to solve this problem? Suppose I were to . . . Or, should I rather . . .' More than likely one would quickly find oneself engaged in working out the problem. Working out *how* to solve the problem *is* working out the problem and when one has solved it one has figured out how to solve it. Of course, one might figure out how to solve a problem without actually solving it. One might not realize one has figured out how and fail to implement or carry one's figuring to completion, or one may make an error in execution thus not solving the problem and not being sure until the solution is discovered or supplied by someone that one has indeed figured out how to do it. If one solves the problem 'right off' first time, one may not even begin to think very much about how to solve it at all. It is like finding something one has been looking for; once one has found it one stops looking.

It is only when we become self-conscious about solving problems that we carry the search further. We wonder how we did it or how we do solve problems. We try to sneak up on ourselves and catch ourselves at it. We try to get people to 'think out loud' so that we might overhear them thinking. But, we are not used to thinking about how we solve problems. Those on whom we would eavesdrop must themselves become self-conscious about their thinking and in this there is every bit as much artificiality as when we try it on our own. It is either contrivance based on inference, 'this must have been what I have been doing' or 'I always do start this way don't I?', or it is a matter of reporting those elements in working out a problem that do not usually get written down — the work that goes on in one's head. If one solves the problem 'right off' there might not even be any discernable unreported work going on in one's head. Then, again, there may be unexpressed work, which, when expressed, may provide data from which to demonstrate a pattern or approach to the solution of problems characteristic of an individual or of different sorts of individuals. But then, this is inference drawn from the expression of what would normally be suppressed behavior. It is inference from overt behavior about behavior. It is observation of human behavior as human behavior, all right, but it represents a reduction of mind to behavior and of mental psychology to behavioral psychology. In the end, I do not think this can be avoided in the scientific study of behavior.

Now, this is not quite the same thing as basing one's analysis of behavior (such as solving problems) on what the individual says _about_ his solving of problems. This is only making, as this is feasible, more of the work involved in arriving at solutions to problems publicly available. When we get into the analysis of behavior by reference to what was going on in people's minds, by reference to mental antecedents, things become rather sticky.

First of all we must get clear about what sorts of things we want to know about behavior. We might be concerned with how an individual solved a particular problem, or how he came to make a particular decision, or why he engages in particular leisure activities, or why he is readily distracted when engaged in purposive activity or is compulsively single-minded in pursuit of any goal once accepted, or what have you. In a broad sort of way we are concerned with behavior from the point of view of purpose of individuals, propensities, dispositions, attitudes as well as the procedures involved in behaving — in doing whatever it is people are doing.

We may be concerned with ordinary or expected behavior or attitudes or dispositions — when people do the sorts of things it is normal for people of their sort to do. And then we might focus on the means by which people (are persuaded to) adopt ordinary purposes and attitudes and the ordinary behavioral means of their expression. It might be interesting to ask people to tell how they came to like doing the things they do or at least why it is they do them. Conceivably, one might discover that they recognize that these are the sorts of things they learned to do or enjoy as they grew up or that these are the things most of their friends and acquaintances do. In this instance the individual reports much the same inferences that an observer might make if he had observed these people over time. The confirmation of the report comes through such observation or through corroboration of other respondents sharing the individual's background and/or present social milieu.

One might think that observation of behavior here might be enough, that one could simply watch what people in a particular group do and understand their behavior. However, one needs to know the meaning of the behavior to the individual and to the group. This may not be directly observable. One may have to ask people about the significance of behavior in order to understand it. Drinking means rather different things to an alcoholic, to a social drinker, to a teenage show-off or a teenage rebel, to the worker on the way home who stops for the nightly one at the pub after knocking off work, to participants in a religious ritual, etc. The nature of the behavior is colored by the motivation, attitudes, construction put on it by those who engage in it. Some of those motivations require considerable inference on the part of observers, and the checking of hypotheses may require asking people questions.

When one asks questions, one must of course, be able to tell when one is getting a straight answer. Suppose someone were to tell an investigator that he drinks because he is an alcoholic, or he drinks because he is a teenager trying to impress his peers. In those instances we are tempted to accept the reports as true because these people are 'telling on' themselves. They are confessing as it were, and there is no obvious advantage to them in confessing. Still, we do not have grounds merely on their report to believe what they say is true. They may be trying to impress the questioner, to capture interest and attention. The teenager might enhance his own sense of maturity by speaking from a mature point of view about his apparently immature behavior. The purported alcoholic may be using the claim as a device for self-chastisement — he is not really an alcoholic but he flogs himself for drinking even occasionally. Or he may use the claim as a means of messing up the questioner, of playing a game with him for a bit of diversion.

What about when the respondent is confused about the meaning of specific behavior to him? He thinks he is giving a straight answer to the question 'why does he drink?' or he is not sure why he drinks and says that he is not sure. Here we have the problem of trying to find out what is going on in someone's mind when that person does not himself know what is going on 'in there'. The two cases are different though. In the one case, the investigator decides the respondent is confused; in the other, the respondent himself claims he is confused.

Suppose in the first case that the respondent claims that he drinks because he likes the taste and because drinking relaxes him. How might the investigator come to suspect that while the respondent probably believes these things there is another, a real reason for his drinking which goes deeper than these? There might be some obvious clues, of course. The man might grimace whenever he downed a shot or he might mix his alcohol in a variety of taste disguises. He might even show more tension as he drinks than beforehand. Then again, he might very well like the taste of the stuff and he might become more sociable, calm, witty, or physically more relaxed with a few drinks in him. How then is one to decide that the man's drinking has deeper meaning than just these? Why would one even suspect that it would have such deeper meaning?

Now, I would not want to take the view, which is often attributed to the mental approach in psychology, that all behavior stems from deep or hidden sources, that all behavior has a hidden meaning deeper than the ordinary sorts of meaning, attitude, purposes, propensity available to ordinary understanding. It seems just plain perverse to insist that people must necessarily be doing what they do for reasons other than, or deeper than, those on which they believe they are acting. People usually do the things they do for the usual sorts of reasons, out of the usual sorts of attitudes and tendencies. We look for hidden or deeper reasons and attitudes and tendencies when there is something unusual about their behavior. And again, usual means usual for particular sorts of people in particular social structures with particular histories. It does seem odd to try to get an individual to seek deeper wellsprings of meaning of *his* engaging in a specific activity common to people of his type with meanings or for reasons common among such people. It seems equally odd for an investigator to ask why a *given individual* does what might be expected unless there is something peculiar about that given individual. Either the behavior is in some way unusual for a member of the group or the member is unusual with respect to the group.

Returning, then, to our example: the drinker who likes the taste and the relaxation afforded by his drinking might be a member of a group in which drinking was severely limited to special occasions. Taste and relaxation might be considered poor reasons for drinking. Then the question of the man's behavior could be a question of his rejection of group norms and this particular expression of that rejection. Or, it could be a question of the strength of his desire for alcohol such that he is willing to face group disapproval for failure to live with group norms. The case might be that while the practice of drinking is not severely limited within the group, this individual imbibes far more than is common among those who enjoy the taste or a bit of relaxation. His reasons for drinking are not good reasons for drinking as much as he does. In any event, the difference between group norms and the individual's behavior often signals a need to probe more deeply. There is some inconsistency to be explained.

The inconsistency may be in the expressed ends or views of the individual. Thus, for example, an investigator may note that the individual's catering to his taste and his desire for relaxation through drinking interferes with his expressed intention to get some job done that requires concentration and a clear head (such as writing a book). That extra drink at dinner may be just what it takes to put off until next morning the writing piously promised this evening. Should this occur with some regularity, an investigator might at least wonder whether the drinking does not indicate an avoidance of writing or of work. Remembering that we posited that the respondent believed the reasons he gave for drinking, we or the investigator might infer that drinking *means* an *unconscious avoidance of work.*

Whether the individual gives straightforward reasons for his behavior or is in the dark about his behavior, the investigator may be led by his behavior or responses to questions to propose some such interpretation of unconscious intent or attitude. Conceivably, when this is brought to the attention of the respondent, he might recognize or admit motivations that he could not previously bring himself to recognize or of which he was totaly ignorant. 'Now that you mention it, it does seem that that is just what I must have been doing', might be the response. What is interesting is that this is an example of inferring motivation or intention from behavior or behavior patterns. What must the state of mind have been or what must it be for the individual to act thus and so? How do we square the inconsistency in behavior and intentions? Restructure the intentions, reinterpret the behavior to provide consistency.

In that case there is the danger of imputing consistency, of imputing motives or a hidden state of mind to the individual that he might not have. Even if one's reinterpretation makes sense to the individual, it still might not be accurate. Thus our drinker might not have wanted to avoid writing his book so much as he enjoyed having that extra drink and loafing a bit. Suppose one had taken the reinterpretation business back a bit deeper into mind and inquired how it was that he wanted to avoid writing the book and posited all sorts of fear of failure or fear of success and notoriety, and then yet further back into early relationships with parents and siblings. A whole edifice might have been built on interpretation of interpretation of interpretation of behavior. Yet our drinker might not have wanted to avoid writing; he just liked his extra drink at dinner and he never could seem to resist the temptation of the moment once he had that first drink in him. Alcohol does affect some people that way, leaving them still sufficiently inhibited to resist the third or fourth drink.

The mental approach to psychology focuses on the meaning of behavior. Behavior can be observed, but the meaning is harder to come by. If the individual cannot provide sufficient meaning for his behavior, if the meaning he provides seems inadequate, then the researcher may try to provide it by the manipulation of the responses to his questions through the apparatus of his interpretive machinery. As interpretation takes over the foreground of the explanatory effort in order to define the behavior observed, mental psychology may succumb to the danger of rationalism.

The very business of construing human behavior as rational, as consistent, as rationally oriented toward achievement of some purpose, constitutes a rationalist bias. I do not want to suggest that human behavior is never any of these things or that it is generally chaotic. But it is often playfully random, serendipitous, purposeless. At times it is just stupid, often dangerously so. It is even inconsistent; at times an individual acts at cross-purposes to his own best interest because he does not know or does not care to know his own best interest. Behavior is often strange, outré, perhaps even deliberately inexplicable. The behavioral scientist, the mental psychologist wishes to make sense out of all sorts of behavior.

This is too easily confused with making all sorts of behavior sensible, with finding reason in what is essentially unreasonable. Perhaps it has its roots in some kind of misunderstanding of Weber's theory of ideal types and the introspective approach to the understanding of human behavior (1949). But Weber was concerned, in part, lest unfamiliar behavior be dismissed or written off as meaningless or intellectually primitive without first seeing whether it could be construed as rational, as purposive. This does not provide the grounds for assuming that all behavior is rational. One even hears talk of what is rational to a madman, what is logical to a schizophrenic, what is reasonable to a paranoid, when in each case one is describing fundamentally irrational, illogical, or unreasonable behavior.

Often such behavior and the mental outlook or 'reasoning' assumes particular forms or patterns. We might be able to describe the ways in which different sorts of schizophrenics 'reason' about things from the things they say and do. Indeed, this is how we classify them as different sorts of schizophrenics. Because *we* can classify them by this behavior and by their states of mind does not mean we can talk about the different forms of rationality of schizophrenics as though these were merely alternative reasoning structures. What 'makes sense' to a nut case does not make sense. We have to remember those scare quotes. The structure for distinguishing among different nut cases is provided by rational people not by nut cases.

Talk about schizos, paranoids and nut cases in general leads rather easily into discussion of psychoanalysis. In one way psychoanalysis fits under the category of the mental approach to psychology and yet in another it fits more properly into the behavioral approach. In the way in which it fits under the mental, it is especially subject to the charge of rationalism.

It is this latter sense that I had in mind when I spoke of interpretation of response to questions getting out of hand. Psychoanalysis has developed into a large body of specialized description and classification schemes and explanatory networks. It has developed a specialized language employing theoretic entities (id, superego, ego, etc.) and hypotheses about the hidden meaning of overt behavior. Initially, psychoanalysis was intended to deal with cases of mental 'imbalance', with disorders of some sort or other. It dealt with behavior that deviated from the norm. It did not explain normal behavior except indirectly. As the clinician sought to uncover the roots of present malfunction in the past experience of the patient, he could generalize about types of malfunction and types of previously associated experiences. From this he or others could begin to generalize normal types of individual histories and competence. One could seek to typify abnormal mental patterns; one could also typify the normal mental pattern. From a conception of mental disorder one might project some sort of reverse image of mental health.

This in itself is a form of rationalization. It is a construction of an ideal type — the normal healthy individual — from a rational consideration of what an individual might be who is free of the different sorts of dysfunctional hang-ups associated with the range of mental illnesses. If a person acts rather strangely, say he cowers in the corner in fear of some invisible force, we know there is some psychological hang-up here. We might want to know what makes him behave that way, what has reduced him to such a state, what has happened to him, or the like. We know by his behavior that he is not normal. But if a person behaves normally, to all outward appearances is normal, how are we entitled to decide that he is not normal or not mentally healthy? We might ask him questions and compare his responses with the sorts of responses we should like to expect from our ideal type mentally healthy person. He might have figured out what sort of game we are playing and then give us the 'good' answers to our questions, so that we have not really got at his true state of mind.

Our questions might then be made more indirect, more abstruse, as we build in special cases with which he might not be familiar. We might ask questions which seem peculiar to him — questions about his relationship to a parent or how he felt about sex when he was a child or some such things. In this way he cannot so easily cheat on his answers. The questions are related to various sorts of psychoanalytic theories about the roots of current behavioral problems. Perhaps normal people have some memories that abnormal people do not have. But, then again, suppose they do have similar memories or feelings about past experience. The pre-interpreted questions (because theory laden) do not entitle us to say in the first instance whether a given behaviorally normal subject is mentally healthy or not, because he might *be* an example of the second instance. We cannot define mental health and illness simply by the way otherwise seemingly healthy individuals answer questions. On the other hand, if there were a set of questions and answers that singled out rather dramatically people with particular mental disorders we should certainly want to be on our guard about the *potential for* mental disorder, for breakdowns in mental health, of someone *apparently* normal who gave those answers to the set of questions.

Psychoanalysis is most subject to the charge of rationalism in the abuse of the concept of 'reaction formation' on the part of some practitioners and theorists. Here interpretation clearly replaces behavioral evidence. For the idea of reaction formation permits contrary interpretations of the same behavior or response from the subject being questioned. It provides the analyst with the choice of assigning meaning to behavior. Suppose, for example, the analyst decides the patient is suffering from anxiety stemming from guilt about his hatred for a parent. The patient insists she loves her mother, calls her on the 'phone regularly, visits with her, enjoys her company and so on. The analyst invokes the idea of reaction formation. The patient does all these things, he says, because she can't face the true state of her feelings for her mother. Had the patient tended to avoid Mom at all costs, the analyst could have come to the same conclusion by not invoking reaction formation. Had the analyst been pushing mother love and dependence on Mom, he could take either of the same reports of the patient as 'evidence' for that interpretation by choosing whether to use the notion of reaction formation. Through the mechanism of interpretation the analyst imposes his meaning on the mind of the patient.

Reaction formation does not explain behavior so much as it explains it away. Perhaps it is hard to imagine a psychoanalyst with his 'preferred fixation of the week' imposing it on his patients in this way. More generally it would be used to handle or erase a discrepancy in the account rendered by a patient where the balance seems to tip in one direction already. It goes one level deeper into interpretation to render an otherwise inconsistent account consistent. The theoretic structure of psychoanalysis is ambiguously tied to behavior. It might wish to emulate the theoretic character of physics, but the generality of the body of physical laws is rather different from the ambiguity of psychoanalytic theory. Psychoanalysis would seem to be the study of theory as behavior, the invention of meaning for behavior rather than the study of behavior as behavior.

There is still that other sense in which psychoanalysis may be taken as more behavioral than 'mental' in approach. The analyst asks his questions, perhaps continuing to use the language and theoretic apparatus of psychoanalysis. But, he is trying to understand the individual's behavior by uncovering more of his behavioral history. Rather than constructing special explanatory devices to explain, he seeks merely to link together syndromes of experience. People who have been raised in certain sorts of environment might receive certain sorts of stimuli and respond in certain sorts of ways and certain of these responses are reinforced in certain ways and in turn invite certain further stimuli, etc. What are hidden and to be uncovered through guided introspection are chains of behavior, not hidden meanings or psychic entities. To use another metaphor, the behavior to be understood is taken as the visible tip of the iceberg, which could not float about the water except as it is supported by the much larger structure below the surface. For the clinician to alter the future development of an individual's behavior not only must he see the visible tip but he must see the whole of which it is but the tip.

The clinician diagnoses and describes by observation and accumulated data about different behavioral structures. To the extent that uniformities in history of particular behavioral types or problems can be established (or at least some useful statistical regularities can be established among the variables in behavioral backgrounds by type), to that extent a step toward understanding of the development of present behavior is taken. Refinement in questioning is possible to elicit differences among individuals with similar experience. The 'structures of icebergs' are charted ever more thoroughly in this way. Perhaps there might even be clues to the sorts of stimuli, experience, behavior likely to influence the further development of an individual along favorable lines. This too may be better understood through the careful observation of clinical practice, treatment strategies and the like. In this way the psychoanalyst seeks to understand human behavior by relating it to human behavior. As he goes back to antecedents, he must rely rather heavily on reports of subjects and perhaps of their friends and relatives — witnesses as it were. As he projects ahead, he may rely on his own and others' experience — indeed on an experimental mode.

The behavioral approach to psychology embraces all three of these — reliance on subject's report, witness report, and experimentation (or, as the jargon has it, evaluation of alternative modes of intervention). Fundamental to the behavioral approach is observation of behavior. Equally fundamental is the effort to eliminate the subject's interpretation of his behavior, or, for that matter, any interpretation of behavior. The behavioral psychologist would avoid the heavily interpretive language of the psychoanalyst. He might note that, to the extent that a psychoanalyst is behaviorally oriented, his theoretic-interpretive language is excess baggage. Or else, it is a witch doctor's mumbo jumbo to make the clinical treatment more 'scientific', imposing, and thereby convincing to the patient. The behavioral psychologist wants to get a handle on behavior in its own terms.

His model is a sort of physical approach to what is more than mere physical behavior. He seeks to grasp the mechanisms of behavior — non-physical mechanisms. In one extreme he appears as a raw empiricist: what happens is what happens. He appears a raw pragmatist: what works to influence behavior, works to influence behavior. 'Let us attend very precisely to what happens in behavior. Let us look very carefully at the impact of our intervention on behavior.' Sophistication comes with detail in observation and description, with the capacity to influence in ever more discriminatory fashion. The greater the detail, the greater the discrimination, the greater the need for sophistication in the management of detail.

Raw empiricism and raw pragmatism are overstatements. To describe behavior as behavior or to talk about what works in altering behavior as a behavioral psychologist requires some conception of what behavior is all about. One must have descriptive categories for classifying behavior. One must have some framework for distinguishing the stages of behavior from initiation through to completion. One needs to distinguish the sorts of things that influence sorts of behavior. The empirical and pragmatic mode in and of themselves do not provide the means for grasping behavior as being of a certain sort, for seeing similar elements in rather different sorts of behavior, or in general, for the development of a general understanding of behavior through the methods of systematic comparison and aggregation of data. Whether the empiricist or pragmatist wishes to admit it or not, his behavioral approach is scientific not merely because he seeks to observe carefully, but because his observation is informed by theory.

His theorizing is not about hidden processes, however. His theorizing is about the structure of behavior. It is gleaned from observation of behavior. And it is imposed on behavior in order to facilitate observation and experimentation.

The behavioral approach to psychology is itself divided into two main approaches, which unfortunately leads to a confusion. One might be characterized as the scientific approach to the study of behavior and the other approach, the technological. The first has developed out of experimental psychology and the second out of industrial psychology with the advent of efficiency engineering. The first seeks to understand behavior by reference to laws such as laws of learning. The second seeks to analyze tasks or productive processes into elements or steps, to reduce complex or gross processes into simple routine procedure. The first would try to discover how complex human behavior arises and operates. The second would seek to replace complex behavior with complex structure of simple behavior. Confusion arises when success in the development of complex structures for the routine completion of tasks is mistaken for an account of how in fact human beings do these tasks. The *re*construction of human behavior is mistaken for the explanation of human behavior. Behaviorism in schooling is solidly based in this confusion. But this is the subject of the next chapter. There is more to be said, yet, about the nature of the behavioral approach to psychology.

The idea of examining behavior as behavior is not so straight-forward as it might first appear. Let us take the second strain of the behavioral approach and ask what it is that the engineer studies when he seeks to simplify some complex task or process. Historically, his concern was for efficiency: the completion of the task with an optimum balance between output or productivity and costs in time, mistakes, money. The environment was the factory or the commercial establishment. The object, of course, was to increase profitability of the operation.

Take a task such as sorting incoming correspondence for routing to appropriate departments in a large catalogue sales firm dealing in thousands of items of merchandise and in thousands of orders each day from customers. The engineer might begin with observation of how the task is initially accomplished, but his attention is very quickly drawn to a consideration of how it ought to be accomplished. He observes behavior for clues as to what could benefit from his special talents, but his forte is the imaginative reorganization of the task, of the work place and even of the tools and equipment with which people work. His focus is on the reorganization of the task. He might propose special alphabetical prefixes in merchandise catalogue numbers which provide the first sorting of orders into broad multi-departmental divisions by one group of sorters. This is followed by further coding for the second round of sorters, and so forth. Sorters may be seated at specially designed work stations where the pigeon holes are arranged in tiers in a semicircular arc to reduce fatigue and increase the volume of material flowing through the station. Pigeon holes may be so placed in the tiers and made of a size to take account of the frequency of ordering of particular kinds of merchandise. In effect, sorting of orders is made more efficient through the breaking down of tasks into sub-tasks or sub-routines of a more specialized nature. The range of behaviors required of any given individual is made more limited. The individual has less to think about, he is more a cog in a behavioral machine than he is a human engaged in intelligent behavior. This is a redefinition of individual behavior into organized group behavior.

Suppose, instead, that the engineer were to apply himself to a case of purely individual behavior: to redesign how someone goes about doing something on his own. The principle is the same as in the previous case. There is some task to be done, some product to be achieved, or some problem to be solved. The behavioral psychologist as engineer analyzes the task or problem into a set of sub-tasks or sub-processes. He reduces to recipe and routine what had previously been accomplished by intuition, feel, taste or some sort of overall intelligent grasp of a problem or task as a whole. What a few people could do by virtue of such endowments, nearly anyone can come to do through recipe and routine. If the mental psychologist's concern with problem solving was to discover how that intelligence operated rather than to find solutions to problems, the behavioral psychologist as engineer is concerned with discovering formulae for solutions to problems to replace the need for intelligence. The behavioral psychologist of this type does not study problem solving behavior in order to understand it. He studies the solving of problems in order to redesign problem solving behavior.

The interest in the redesign of behavior is not limited to the setting of sub-routines for the wider dissemination of the capacity for solving otherwise intellectually demanding problems. Behavior modification[6] represents the engineering approach to the treatment of all sorts of behavioral disorders or dysfunctions. Indeed, what might appear to the mental approach psychologists as surface evidence of neuroses, psychoses, or phobias of various sorts to be treated by psychoanalysis and clinical counseling are viewed on the behavioral approach at the surface as behavior to be modified by redesign. The dysfunctional or disordered behavior is evaluated as such by reference to some goal or objective that the individual has (or perhaps ought to have). The over-eater really would rather be slim and attractive than fat and sloppy. The aggressive unruly child really would rather be liked by his peers and have lots of friends than shunned and avoided. 'See how eating all the time is dysfunctional?' 'See how being such a nasty, sneaky, bully is dysfunctional?' (Of course the nasty, sneaky, bully may enjoy being just that.) 'Now let's see if we can substitute other behavior for the dysfunctional behavior.' Perhaps it is too much to expect an immediate change of behavior all at once (it *is* so tempting to say change of character, but that would not be true to the behavioral approach in question).

The behavioral psychologist designs a program of specific goals and tasks. He breaks 'eating to be healthy, trim and handsome' into a set of habits — into a routine. He prescribes things to do at eleven o'clock so that one replaces that eleven o'clock craving for food with the anticipation of engaging in the eleven o'clock non-eating activity. For the nasty brat he provides a schedule of nice things to do for

people, 'share candy with Tommy, help someone do something, etc.'
The idea is that by substituting specific instances of functional
behavior the individual is not faced with the overwhelming prospect
of changing character. He is given a routine that will in the aggregate
have him behave as the sort of person he wants to (or ought to) be.

Now this is the way it is supposed to work, but there is the
problem of motivation. The model assumes behavior directed toward
the successful completion of a task or accomplishment of an ultimate
objective through the adoption of short-term behavioral steps. If an
individual has the will to achieve the ultimate goal, he might master
the self-discipline necessary to engage in and carry out the long-term
process. If he has doubts about achieving the ultimate objective, or if
he has mixed feelings about achieving it, or if he is not so committed
to it as he is supposed to be, then he may need something to stiffen
his flagging will, or even to provide it where it is lacking. There may
have to be a system of short-term pay-offs for short-term
accomplishments (or even penalties for short-term failure or
backsliding — as in denial of privilege, for example, when what is
viewed as privilege by the engineer is viewed by the subject as his
right or due). The rewards may be through verbal praise and
reinforcement or in more material form. In any event, the behavior
modifier is no longer working purely on the engineering or
technological mode. He has crossed over into the more classical
mode of behavioral psychology as he focuses his attention on the
stimulation and/or the reinforcement of desirable (or desired)
behavior.

The scientific approach to behavioral psychology is characterized
not so much by the reconstruction and reorganization of behavioral
tasks as by the examination of the sources and conditions affecting
the adoption, maintenance, and termination of various sorts of
behavior. What sorts of things do people do? How do they come to do
those things? Why do people stop doing some things rather than
continue to do them? The answers must come from the observation
of the influence of the behavior of individuals on other individuals,
from the influence of environmental circumstance on the behavior of
individuals or on some combination of these. The answers must be
out in the open, not hidden in physiological processes or mysterious
depths of psyche. The problem of motivation, of the will of the
subject to alter his behavior, as it was raised for behavior modification
is retranslated as a matter of discovering the circumstances in which

and what must be done to arrange those circumstances so that the individual does behave appropriately. If there is to be psychological theory it should be of the sort where variables indicating directly observable phenomena are to be linked to one another in a structure of laws or law-like generalizations. At the very least there should be good statistical predictive grounds establishing linkages between environmental conditions, behavioral experience and the adoption, or maintenance, or termination of specific sorts of behavior.

The scientific sort of behavioral psychologist, then, must identify some kind of behavior and account for it. He has available to him for investigation the whole range of behavioral repertoires discussed in the last chapter. He might pick out particular social customs or amenities and describe the process of acculturation — the ways in which parents teach their children, the ways in which others in the environment discourage alternative behavior and encourage the favored behavior. He might generalize from his descriptions about particular child-rearing practices or social practices tending to promote, maintain or discourage specific behavioral practice in individuals and he might contrive means to test these generalizations. He might seek to discover whether some stimuli or reinforcements are more crucial than others to the adoption of the behavior in question, by comparing individuals, say, whose reinforcement histories differ or by examining the reinforcement histories of individuals of varying levels of observed commitment to the behavior in question. There may be careful selection of control and experimental groups such that social background, cultural background, age, maturity level, etc. may be matched so that relevant behavioral experience may be related to behavioral practices of the subjects involved. Or behavioral experience may be contrived for appropriately matched groups to test experimentally the effects of particular intervention practices or changes in behavioral environment on specific sorts of behavior of the subjects.

Now, we often stop far short of this in practice. We are often happy with only a gross sort of behaviorism in which the noting of difference in behavioral practice or repertoire is related to differences in environmental, social, economic, racial or maturational circumstance of subjects. This is to explain behavior not by behavior but by the non-behavioral identity of the members of the groups. There may very well be differences in the behavioral experiences of members of these sorts of different groups, but a scientific approach to behavioral psychology is at best gratuitous in its reasoning if it only infers such differences from the differences in the behavior to be accounted for. If a researcher points out, what may be interesting to note, say that lower social class children of some ethnic backgrounds are more likely to engage in certain forms of criminal behavior then lower social class children of other specifiable ethnic backgrounds, he has related behavioral difference to other variables. But these other variables are not yet behavioral variables. In one sense he has accounted for difference in behavior, but not in terms of behavior.

The behaviorist who would explain human behavior as human behavior must go on to examine the ways in which the behavior in question is influenced by group membership. It might turn out that members of certain groups do have different behavioral histories from members of other groups. This still is not enough. The differences in behavioral history must be shown to make a difference to the behavior under examination. It might then turn out that there are such differences. It might even turn out that the occurrence of the behavior in question might be directly related to certain sorts of behavioral antecedents. Those individuals from whatever group who have had certain sorts of behavioral experience, who have been influenced by certain sorts of practice, might turn out to be those who exhibit the behavior of interest to the investigator. The relative frequencies of such practices among members of various groups thus account for the frequencies by group in the target behavior.

This is the behavioral ideal. The political scientist who explains someone's voting pattern by reference to his income, parent's income, ethnic group, parent's political affiliation and the like, might call himself a behavioralist,[7] but on this view he accounts for behavior by reference to environment, at best, rather than explaining the mechanisms of the behavioral influence of people in that behavior on his voting pattern. Perhaps the political behavioralist should not have to do this. After all he does not pretend to be a psychologist. Should he attempt to uncover the behavioral mechanisms influencing voting patterns, he would be a sort of crossbreed political scientist-behavioral psychologist. Perhaps some of those who engage in studies of political socialization are doing just this sort of thing (with or without the psychologist's license). Perhaps anthropologists concerned with the cross-cultural study of the effects of child-rearing practices on the behavior of children and ultimately on adult social practices are doing much the same sort of things.

If the mechanisms for ensuring specific sorts of behavior were understood, then it is conceivable, at least, that institutions might be so devised, social structures might be put into place, social practices might be so designed that people could be made to do the sorts of things they need to do in the aggregate to develop and maintain a happy and healthy society. It is just such a society that Plato would have had managed by the philosophical elite. It is just such a society that B. F. Skinner advocates in *Walden Two* (1948) and *Beyond Freedom and Dignity* (1971), a society managed by the behavioral engineer. Skinner believes that the mechanisms for ensuring human behavior are understood and that such a society is feasible.

Now, this would seem to make behavioral psychology the queen of the social sciences. It reduces the critique of social institutions, political, economic, whatever, to questions of behavioral engineering. It presumes to generalize the design of society from the principles underlying the socialization of the individual. But psychology is not political science nor is it economics, and there is no point in confusing things that are different.

The source of this confusion lies in the ambiguity of the notion of behavior. The behavioral repertoire is more than a mere bag of specific practices engaged in semi-automatically. Much of human behavior is exceptionally complex in the variety of responses available to the same (sorts of) stimuli. To know the principles of human learning or human behavior is to know both too little and too much. Since they underlie the learning of all behavior, they tell us very little about the specific antecedents of any given piece of behavior. A knowledge of specific antecedents of specific behavior is only as good as its certificate of dependability (its statistical support). The edifice of behavioral psychology is built on the provision of such certificates of dependability and these can be given, in the main, to the portion of the behavioral repertoire that is semi-automatic.

But, there is also the part of the behavioral repertoire that is not so automatic. Individuals have learned capacities to engage in varieties of activities, to pursue complex and often conflicting goals, to enlarge upon the behavior that has been programmed into them and to adapt to opportunities and changes in the environment in all sorts of imaginative ways. In every carefully devised structure to constrain individual behavior there are loopholes and there are people to find them and exploit them. We may understand the principles by which a child learns a language and still 'wonder what that boy will say next'. As I mentioned earlier, the more confining, the more limiting of the range of acceptable behavior in a given society, the more strictly sanctions are applied to suppress undesired behavior, then the less likely imaginative behavior will be exhibited. The more liberal the exercise of imagination is permitted, the more culturally pluralistic the society, the more alternatives are presented, then the more likely the exercise of individual options in the development of behavior patterns.

It may seem that whatever a person does he must have learned how to do. There must have been a proper set of conditions and the appropriate behavioral influence for him to learn to do whatever he has learned to do. The laws of learning, if there really are any, must undergird whatever learning of whatever behavior occurs. Still, everything a person does need not have been taught him, nor need he have learned how to do it prior to his successfully doing it. He might learn how to do it in the very doing of it for the very first time. Indeed, he may not even be sure about how he does it, but he just does it. Some people, for example, are extremely witty conversationalists. They always seem to come up with an apt phrase or a funny retort that makes a conversation sparkle. They do these things but they do not know how they do them, nor can they discover that they have learned to do them. They have learned the same language as the others with whom they converse. It is only gratuitous to insist that there must have been an especially appropriate set of environmental conditions and behavioral influence in their backgrounds as compared to the others. One must be able to pinpoint just those conditions and influences and relate these to their saying just those things in just those circumstances. After all, are we to account for verbal behavior of a certain sort or for certain specific verbal behavior? We might conceivably come up with the former, but it seems inconceivable that we could come up with the latter. 'John Jones is likely to be a sparkling conversationalist' may follow upon observation of his behavioral history, etc. 'John Jones will say "*xxx*" on the occasion of someone else saying "*zzz*" ' is hardly credible.

Perhaps this sort of criticism is too strong. Science is not fortune telling, after all. Perhaps it is enough to be able to relate present *sorts* of behavior to their behavioral antecedents. 'John Jones was rewarded for having made witty remarks as a boy and this encouraged him to continue to make witty remarks.' Of course, on the other hand, he may have been discouraged or regularly 'shot down', but being 'irrepressible' he continued to sharpen his skills at repartee . . . The point is that in either case we have not explained his tendency to think of the witty remarks in the first place. Some people are imaginative, insightful, and bright — more so than others. We may be able to calculate the likelihood of finding them represented in various numbers in populations of different sorts, but again this does not account for what made them that way.

The behavioral approach to psychology assumes either that they were made that way by their behavioral histories, or that they can be constrained to behave along certain lines by appropriately designed environmental conditions. The emphasis is on the plasticity of the individual, on the malleability of the individual. Some less doctrinaire behaviorists took a much less extreme position. Thorndike insisted on the notion of innate or inherent differences among individual people, on differences especially in intelligence (Joncich, 1962, pp. 118-26). Individuals, in his view, contribute to the development of their own behavior and any scientific approach to behavioral psychology would have to come to terms with this fact. At any rate, laws general enough to account for behavior in people of varying degrees of intelligence would be too general to account for specific sorts of behavior. Consider the analogy: the law of gravity accounts for things coming to earth but does not tell the police detective whether he is investigating an accident, a suicide, or a murder — 'Did he fall, did he jump, or was he pushed?' To know the most up to date version of 'The law of effect' or 'The law of exercise' does not tell us what behavior in the repertoire will be put into effect or exercised in the political or economic spheres. Still, in the absence of evidence of other causes of death, the detective's awareness of the force of gravity does reduce the mysterious character of the victim's demise considerably. Similarly, the mysteries of accounting for human behavior may be considerably reduced as we take one or another sort of behavioral stance. When it comes to the business of schooling we are constrained to do so. After all, we are then consciously engaged in shaping behavior. While some may seek laws of behavior in order to restructure the conditions, social institutions, practices, reinforcing the 'good' society, in schooling we are more conspicuously concerned to restructure the behavior of the individual directly. We must provide his environment. We must establish the conditions and the things teachers do that lead to the development of the appropriate behavioral repertoires of the student. And in the name of behaviorism we can do this more, or less, intelligently.

NOTES

1. Available from Human Relations Area Files, Inc., New Haven, Conn.
2. See, for example, R. L. Thorndike's review (1969) of Rosenthal and Jacobson, *Pygmalion in the Classroom* (1968).
3. See Humphreys (1968).
4. For discussion of problem solving see Kleinmuntz (1966).
5. The position that intelligent behavior is one thing and not two is perhaps best advanced by Ryle (1949).
6. For an overview of behavior modification see Thoresen (1973).
7. See Charlesworth (1962); some political scientists have tended to evade nasty charges of behaviorism by adopting the disguise of behavioralism.

CHAPTER 4

Behaviorism and Educational Program

When it comes to the practice of education, we are all behaviorists. Whatever these things may be, there are things that we would have children learn. We care enough that they learn these things to send them to schools or at least to put them into the way of getting what it is we want them to have in knowledge, attitudes, skills, feelings . . . We might emphasize the provision of a special setting or environment with or without specially designed materials or social structure, or we may emphasize special forms of instruction, or some combination of these. The learning of what is to be learned is important enough that we try to arrange things so that it is learned. We have to do things and our pupils have to do things in order that they may learn. The only way we can tell what they have learned or that they have learned is by having them do things to give us evidence of their learning. There is no magic way of getting inside the pupil to make it happen or tell that it is happening. In a rather common sense way of looking at the business, schooling is a behavioral enterprise.

Is the enterprise of schooling, at bottom, a scientific enterprise? We are obviously concerned with the business of how to teach this or that, how to improve the learning of something or other, how to tell whether some procedure is better than another, how to tell whether students are learning or what they are learning. All of these common sense questions about the effectiveness of the enterprise, all of these 'how to' questions, may be pursued in a rigorous fashion as the development of a technology of education. They are engineering sorts of questions.

In the last chapter a distinction was made between a scientific approach to behavioral psychology and the engineering approach. I claimed that the confusion of the two is fundamental to the development of behaviorism in schooling. The scientific status of the enterprise of schooling will be made clear with the explanation of what I mean by this claim. I have chosen the word 'status' quite deliberately. While one can trace the roots of the quest for a science of schooling out of the development of behavioral psychology, much of current practice in educational research seems to work from the other direction. Common sense 'how to' questions may be elevated to questions of technology by their attachment to the advancement of learning theory. The confusion of science and technology in behavioral psychology is further compounded by the confusion of technological questions of schooling with questions of psychology — scientific or technological. We might best begin unravelling these confusions by looking again at the relationship of science and technology.

The Construction of Knowledge and the Knowledge of Construction

Students training to become teachers are generally required to receive instruction in psychology. Usually this instruction is given under the heading of educational psychology. Often even more basic instruction in the introduction to psychology is demanded as a prerequisite for the educational psychology course. Teachers in training as well as experienced teachers are often heard to complain that they do not see the need for such study in their day-to-day concerns with the problems of teaching. Such study is too abstract, they say. It does not really tell them much about how to teach thirty children to read by the end of the term, or how to teach Johnny his arithmetic. Perhaps as R. S. Peters said some time ago, psychologists have more to learn from teachers about education than teachers have to learn from psychologists (1959, chap. 10).

In fact psychology, even educational psychology, is too abstract as a subject of study to be of much direct everyday practical use to teachers. Peters was correct in his assessment. But this is not an indictment of psychology or even of educational psychology. It does not, as Peters thought it did, call for a greater attentiveness on the part of psychologists to day-to-day problems of teaching in school. Psychology is a properly abstract or general study. Teaching is a practical business.

The distinction is easily obscured in the once popular terminology of 'pure' and 'applied' science. The pure scientist seeks knowledge for its own sake. The applied scientist seeks knowledge in order to solve a particular technical problem, in order to advance the practice of some occupation. The most common models are in physics and chemistry. The pure physicist or chemist seeks to uncover the nature of matter and of the universe. He wants to know what there is and how things are related by natural processes. The applied physicist wants to use that knowledge to build something, to alter things. He invents radio, develops television, then color television and refinements of replay, slow motion, etc. The applied chemist might be concerned with the creation of membranes of appropriate composition for the process of water desalinization. The advancement of technology is not explicit in a knowledge of pure science. If I were to gather together a set of materials of various sorts that might be used to build a number of different objects, a knowledge of physics or chemistry would not in itself tell me what might be made with them. My experience with such objects as things with which to construct, my imagination based on such experience, my interest in making certain sorts of things would help. And it is through subsequent experimentation that I find out what I can construct, how I can best do it out of the materials at hand, whether I need some other materials and of what sort, and perhaps whether things I want to do can be done at all given *the* or *my* present knowledge of the art of construction.

As any construction engineer or architect knows, whatever he builds or whatever he designs must conform to the laws of physics. The bridge that collapses, just as the bridge that stands in the teeth of the gale, conforms to the laws of physics. The skyscraper office building in Boston, Massachusetts with the tendency to shed its windows is not an example of a breakdown in pure science. One would not fault the architect or the engineer for their grounding in pure physics in the latter case. It would be somewhat misleading, though true, to say that one made an error in applied physics, here. For applied physics here means a knowledge of engineering and architectural design — all the experimentation and familiarity with materials and technique that have led to general principles of construction and design that with all its measurement and calculation is more art than science, albeit more the art of the artisan than of the artist.

Now, pure and applied science are distinguished primarily by the concern with the improvement of knowledge for its own sake as against the improvement of the practice of some art. There is still some overlap here. The architect does not want to design a structure that will collapse. At the very least he would be aided in his work if he were to know enough physics to recognize limiting conditions on his designs: he cannot fly in the face of gravity in building a bridge; he should understand the principle of the lever. Advances in pure physics or chemistry provide him with new ways of looking at his materials, perhaps even with new materials. On the other side of the coin, advances in applied science often lead to the uncovering of new phenomena yet to be understood by pure science or to be utilized as tools in the advancement of pure science. The people engaged in one or the other activity as their central occupation may, in the course of their work, change functions. Indeed, this is most likely where the people in both areas have a similar grounding in the fundamentals of the scientific area. The applied scientist may have an insight into a problem of pure theoretic interest which arises in the course of his work. The pure scientist may solve a problem of application in order to be able to make particular experiments crucial to his work. After all, both operate more or less directly in an experimental enterprise. The test of theory, as of practice, is a matter of observing what happens when one does things.

Let us bring in our two sorts of behavioral psychologists here. Not surprisingly, the scientific approach has already been characterized as motivated by an interest in pure science — the advancement of knowledge for its own sake. And the engineering approach is easily recognized as applied. If there are laws of behavior established by the pure behavioral psychologist it would be useful for the applied behaviorist to know them. There is little point in trying to get people to do what they cannot be made to do. There may be some general notions of human behavior to be exploited in practice. Looking the other way, the applied behaviorist may come up with some observations that lead to larger generalizations about human behavior. His primary task, though, is to improve some aspect of human behavior. He may be an applied behavioral psychologist in general, but he must work in specifics. Of course, he may come up with some general procedural rules about the analysis of applied behavioral problems or some generalizations about strategies for dealing with them. The state of knowledge in behavioral psychology may be such that the distinction between the pure and the applied approaches may be harder to maintain, as practitioners grope for theory or among theories.

Still, if behavioral scientific theory is to have any bearing at all on the business of schooling it is through the intermediary of applied behavioral psychology. This is neither a claim against general psychology in the education of teachers nor is it support for the inclusion of educational psychology. An introduction to the science of psychology is not particularly useful to the ordinary working classroom teacher concerned with planning what to do in the practice of teaching. By definition, pure psychology is not practical. It is misleading to teachers to pretend that it is practical and it is unfair to suggest it to them. For then, when they do not see how to apply it in practice, they are likely to be frustrated and perhaps even suspicious of their own intellectual competence. At the same time we might wish to promote the study of psychology for entrants into teaching on the grounds that those who would educate others ought themselves to be well educated — that teachers ought to know more than what to teach and how to teach it. Moreover, while psychology — as science — will not tell the teacher what to do in reading class at nine o'clock the next day, it is especially appropriate that teachers have some grasp of the general principles of learning and laws of behavior. These provide *part* of the context for a general overview of the nature of the teacher's chosen profession. They help to define the business in which so many of us are engaged.

What about educational psychology? If the teacher is presented with psychology as science under the heading of educational psychology, then much the same thing could be said about its usefulness or desirability in a teacher's education. If it is exceedingly abstract or general in treatment, if it is mainly concerned with learning theory based on animal experimentation, if it deals primarily with preschool behavioral development of children or non-school environmental influence — in short with all manner of topics other than how children learn in schools and how one can best teach them in schools the sorts of things teachers are supposed to teach children in schools — then it is difficult to justify on grounds of hard practicality. It may be helpful for teachers to know some of these things, but it would be more helpful to know the practical bearings of these things on the practice of teaching. If the study of educational psychology is construed as the study of how particular things are best learned and taught in schools it would obviously be an essential ingredient in the preparation of the teacher. It would be nothing less than the study of the practice of schooling.

Is it any more than that? Suppose people were to engage in the systematic study of classroom teaching and learning. I do not mean some sort of simple-minded time and jaw motion study of teacher/student originated communication. I do not mean the development of some pretentious curriculum theory or equally pretentious theory of teaching. The ideas of theory in the scientific sense are misapplied here altogether. I mean purely and simply that researchers investigate the ways in which particular teachers teach particular subjects to particular children. Let them ask children and their teachers what sorts of things are hard to teach and to learn. Let them observe teachers teaching children to read, for example, and let them watch and listen to children struggling to learn to read. Let them compare different approaches with appropriate attention to differences in teachers and students and appropriate experimental controls. In sum, let them make the study of schooling a study in its own terms. Since we are stuck with the view from the outside, then it must needs be a behavioral study. It is, as described here thus far, a technological sort of study with no pretentions to more than this. I do not mean to suggest that such research does not go on. My point is that one need not be a technological sort of behavioral psychologist to engage in it.

If psychologists have more to learn from teachers than teachers have to learn from psychologists, we might still, as Peters pointed out (1959), need to become much clearer about what might be learned from teachers. The systematic study of teaching and learning is not just a matter of codifying the common sense observations of teachers about their business. Much of *common* sense in any sphere is interlaced with commonly accepted nonsense. Someone must cull out the nonsense and codify and develop what is sensible. There is no reason in the nature of the work why this someone must be the representative either of the field of psychology or of some new 'discipline'. There is no special reason why school people should be concerned for the advancement of psychology. Why should they need a new intermediary discipline for the advancement of the study of schooling?

If one wants to improve the teaching of some subject in the curriculum, one is not interested in abstract knowledge about teaching for its own sake. One is interested in the improvement of teaching of that subject so that it will be better learned by children. One may wish to improve children's learning of all the things they are to learn, but that is no license to treat all the things they are to learn as being of a piece. Children are to learn different things, specific things. Children do not learn in the abstract: they learn to read, to write, to do rather different sorts of mathematics; they learn to draw, to paint, to make things out of wood or metal, to dance, to ride bicycles, to speak their own language, to speak a foreign language, to do chemistry or physics, to think historically — so many different things. Perhaps these things present common learning difficulties, perhaps there are teaching approaches that work in several areas. Perhaps children of some backgrounds have common learning problems in some subjects. Before one can talk about such commonalities, one must know what the things are that may be compared to find commonalities.

The starting place is in an understanding of each particular subject to be learned. This raises some very large questions of philosophy as well as of the several subjects of knowledge. It also raises very specific questions of a practical nature. The larger questions deal with the nature of mathematics, or of historical knowledge or 'what constitutes a knowledge of chemistry?' When we ask what one should know about mathematics or chemistry or history at the completion of one's secondary school work or general education, our questions are still rather large as they imply a conception of the appropriate distinction between what we think 'everyone should know' and what we think those with more specialized study should know. The distinction is a practical distinction, if it is to define the curriculum of the schools. Presumably we should require the schools to provide instruction in what everyone ought to know about particular subjects.

When we ask just what is involved in the knowledge of chemistry, or algebra, or woodworking, or whatever subject is expected of the generally educated, we indeed get down to rather practical questions. For the answers to these questions set the specific objectives of teachers and students in the day-to-day business of schooling. These set the details of what teachers must teach and students must learn.

The special character of behaviorism in schooling is best (or worst) illustrated in the increasing scientism in the defining of the school curriculum. It should become clear from the discussion that follows that one need not know any psychology to be this sort of behaviorist. And yet, one can also see the roots in the engineering approach to behavioral psychology.

Behavioral Definition of Educational Objectives

Imagine you have been given an engineering problem. The schools are to turn out certain sorts of products — young people who know things (history, mathematics, physics . . .), who have some vocational skills, who have sensitivities of an aesthetic sort, who have requisite understanding of the rights and responsibilities of membership in society, etc. Immediately, if you are a good engineer you want some more specific description of the product. What are you to deliver if you are going to deliver the goods? You call in a philosopher who waxes eloquent about the nature of mathematics or about the concepts of individualism and social responsibility. All well and good, you think, but what do we want of young adults? Should they be able to expound at length about these things as the philosopher has done? Should something less than that be required of them? Are we to build Fords or Rolls Royces, ordinary citizens or philosophers?

Now an engineering approach may be taken to be the determination of what might be required of ordinary people. One can do research to find out the sorts of things that most people know about various subjects. There is research to be done on the differences among various sorts of people and the ease or difficulty with which they learn various sorts of things. There is no point in requiring the schools to spend time teaching everyone what most people are not going to learn, anyhow. Researchers might properly try to find just what level of knowing is likely to be achieved in most areas of schooling by various segments of the population. Another sort of research might try to discover how much knowledge in what areas is necessary or useful on the part of all members of a society — what sorts of knowledge of what sorts of things in mathematics, for example, might be required generally for individuals to get on as workers, consumers, voters, etc. Perhaps the researchers might try to establish the benefits to society and its individual members of increased levels of knowledge or education beyond previously necessary levels — say that the more educated the citizenry, the greater the productivity of the economy and the better the standard of living (see Schultz, 1971).

In the end, though, the ultimate decision on the definition of the curriculum, or the desired product of schooling, is more than an engineering decision. The engineer might tell us what is possible in the way of schooling and in the usefulness or necessity of alternative levels and sorts of schooling to various social ends. But the engineer has no special qualification as engineer for deciding on those social ends or the proper role of schooling as a social institution to achieve those ends. This may be forgotten by some in the setting of behavioral objectives for schooling. Neither science nor engineering have special qualifications for the setting of society's goals.

Still the problem remains: how is an engineer to translate society's or a community's or even the local gadfly's general curricular objectives into terms specific enough to determine what it is that people are to do in school? The answer of 'behavioral definition' is quite simple. Describe just what it is that one expects appropriately schooled people to be able to do in each of the subjects of their schooling. If one wants them to know mathematics, list the various forms and levels of mathematics one wants them to know and specify just which sorts of operations under each of these headings they are expected to be able to perform. Convert 'knowledge of mathematics' into a list of specific 'behaviors'. One who does a, b, c . . . knows X. 'Knows X' is defined by 'does a, b, c . . .'. The automotive engineer converts the objective of 'good acceleration' into 'goes from 0 to 60 miles per hour in 5.2 seconds'; 'ease of handling' becomes 'turns within a radius of x feet with Y degree of sway and Z speed'. Just as there are automotive 'specs', we now have educational 'specs'.

The establishment of such educational specifications may be developed for every subject at every level of the curriculum from the kindergarten on up. If we specify what it is that children are to be able to do at the end of kindergarten — identify colors, numbers, letters, put on own outer clothing, engage in the following individual as well as group activities (list), etc. — then the teacher knows what it is she is trying to accomplish with each child. Her objectives are set in the description of the behavior that the child should exhibit. If she can get each child to do thus and so, then the doing of it is evidence of her and their accomplishment. If the chemistry teacher has a list of experiments and exercises to be performed by the members of her group of sixteen year olds by the end of the term, then she knows and we know what she is about in teaching chemistry. The mystery of teaching school subjects is replaced by explicit formulation.

The literature teacher can no longer get by with an objective of 'teaching young people to appreciate the joys of reading'. 'Appreciating the joys of reading' must be translated into a set of specific items of behavior. What does one do who appreciates the joys of reading? The history teacher who wants his students to 'develop a sense of history' must specify just what someone does who has a sense of history. He must define his objective in terms of the behavior of his students. What the teacher is trying to do in teaching is to get the students *to do those things* that would serve as *evidence* of their having gained an appreciation of literature or of their having developed a sense of history.

Behavioral definition of educational objectives makes a virtue out of the fact that in teaching we are limited to the view from the outside. As we cannot get into our students' heads to see what they have learned, they must provide us in their behavior with evidence of what they have learned. We have to decide what is to count as evidence of their having learned what it is we intend that they should learn. If we cannot specify what we would take to be appropriate evidence, then how can we justify the claim to be teaching them anything? Behavioral definition of objectives does not define what we as teachers do in the classroom, it defines what students are to do as a result of instruction, of being in classrooms under our direction. It does not define instruction; it defines the test of instruction. The ultimate justification (but not the only justification) of what the teacher does in the classroom is in what the student learns. The teacher who asks, 'How do I know I am teaching?' is given the questions in reply, 'How do you know you are teaching *what*?' and 'What would count as evidence that you have taught *that*?' and then is told that these are really only one question.

There is a rather healthy empiricism in all this. For years, we have listened to critic after critic inside and outside of schooling complaining about ritualism in teaching, the mindlessness of the whole business. We do the things we do as teachers because these are the things teachers do. We require our students to do the sorts of things that students are required to do. But now we are asked to consider whether all this does, in fact, have a bearing on whether our students learn what it is we expect them to learn. At the very least we should know what it is we expect them to learn and be able to tell whether they have learned it. And if they have not learned it we had better figure out some other way of getting them to learn it; we had better change what we do, or what we have them do in the classroom, for something is not working right. Or else we have to change what it is we expect them to do as a result of our teaching. We might even give up some of our objectives as unspecifiable and therefore untestable, or unteachable.

There are difficulties in this idea as well. One sort of ritualism may be exchanged for another. The translation of subjects in the curriculum into behaviors of pupils may be done in a rather simple minded fashion. For the non-specific objectives of 'knows algebra' a teacher might substitute 'passes the final examination in algebra with a grade of D or better'. This is not very specific, but it is a behavioral definition. More specific might be: 'passes an examination on the textbook used in algebra class, scoring better than half on each section of the text.' This avoids the chore of writing down or summarizing a good deal of the text in listing behavioral objectives. But it is no more than a formalization of what the algebra teacher might have been doing for years. The added step of actually writing down the summary of the text adds nothing but the paper filled up in the process. If 'appreciates the joys of literature' is translated as 'writes an essay demonstrating an appreciation of the joys of literature', this is behavioral definition but the translation has all the fuzziness of the original. If it is translated as 'demonstrates an appreciation of the richness and variety of literature in the recognition of sources of quotations from (list) on examination and renders a critical comparison of the following works of (list)' then there is greater specification, but, again, whatever the teacher has been doing can be so translated. So long as the teacher has been examining students, having them produce some purported evidence of their learning related to the subject of study, whatever the teacher has been doing can be converted to the formulae of the behavioral definition of educational objectives. The value of what is done by the teacher over the course, the value of what the students are expected to do by the end of the course, may remain as obscure as before the conversion. The substance of schooling may stay the same with a new set of rituals. Traditional practice is no longer to be supported as traditional; it is now 'scientific'. There is nothing in the idea of behavioral definition of educational objectives that *requires* enlightenment in the setting of such objectives.

There is nothing in the idea that *requires* empirical evaluation of teaching by reference to the objectives. In part, this is because of a peculiar insulation of objectives from teaching practice. The engineering specifications for a product do not tell us how to build it, they only tell us what we want built into the product. If teachers can decide individually or arbitrarily what behavioral evidence counts as student learning of their subjects, then, if their students generally exhibit such evidence, the teachers can claim that they 'must have been doing something right', whatever they were doing. It could very well be that most of what they were doing had little demonstrable impact on student performance, but that student pre-exam grinding away at the books and practice in other exams, or conference with students who had taken such exams earlier — these made the difference. Teachers and students might yet believe that the teacher was teaching them and be rather hesitant to give up all or most of that classroom work in favor of the grinding, the practice, and the conferring. Should some sorts of students have difficulty in meeting the objectives, teachers might (and some do) point out that there must be some special reason, some deficiency in prior development whether for educational, cultural or innate intellectual reasons that have not fitted the students to benefit from the teacher's instruction.

Thus far, all that has been shown is that behavioral definition of educational objectives is rather easily made trivial and that it need not lead to the improvement of teaching at all. I strongly suspect that in practice this business will suffer from both defects. Teachers are a conservative lot when it comes to the practice of their trade, perhaps rightfully so. All sorts of new rituals and jargon have come and gone over the years. The teacher is beset by conflicting demands to promote standards, to teach *all* children of all backgrounds, to concentrate on solid academic work, to promote understanding, to seek out and educate the gifted, the mentally handicapped, to educate for character, to be more scientific in schooling, to be more like the creative artist in teaching. From time to time different demands are emphasized and the emphases wax and wane in cycles. The maintenance of teacher sanity would tend to favor interpretation and absorption of these demands into the ongoing teaching practices. Where demands conflict, teachers are vulnerable to complaint by someone. If whatever the teacher is doing can be explained as in conformity with whatever the demands, the less vulnerable the teacher. But this only tells us that behavioral definition is likely to go the way of so many other purported improvements in schooling. It would not really be taken seriously.

There is yet the potential for harm, if the idea is taken too seriously. Earlier, I said that behavioral definition defines not instruction but rather the test of instruction. Subsequently, I showed that even the latter may be avoided. Now, I want to show how the test of instruction may indeed be taken to define instruction. The objectives may define the curriculum too narrowly and they may determine teaching practice in too rigid and mechanical a fashion. Both faults stem from a very old sort of practice in schooling, one that has long been decried under the heading of 'teaching to the examination'.

Testing and Teaching

It should come as no surprise that the setting of educational objectives in behavioral terms has its roots in the field of educational testing (see Bloom, 1956). The effort to make schooling more scientific required the specification of the outcomes of schooling in observable terms. The organization of the effort to evaluate teaching and learning led to the development of organized structures describing, in layers of increasing detail, what sorts of things students do if they have attained particular levels of proficiency in the various subjects of schooling. That curriculum and teaching method might be determined in this fashion has been promoted on three counts. It is promoted on grounds that its roots in the field of educational testing — the most quantitative branch of educational psychology — make this scientific (never mind the confusion of science and technology). To develop curriculum and teaching method enhances one's claim that schooling has a basis in science. (For some reason school people feel that this is important and are especially eager to claim some sort of parity with medicine, the practice of which is supposed to rest on a basis in the physical sciences.) It is promoted as efficient. Here, then, techno-logical roots of educational psychology come to the fore in a confused fashion. Never mind that product specification is not the same as productive technology. And it is promoted as providing account-ability. Teachers and schools may be more readily held to account for what they produce when the product can be described in objectively observable terms. I shall deal with these grounds as I proceed to a discussion of, first, testing and the curriculum, followed by testing and teaching.

Testing and the curriculum. 'Evaluation' as it is euphemistically termed, or exams may undermine the curriculum at two levels: the various subjects to be included in a school's program of studies and the sorts of things to be included within each subject. There may be some philosophical commitment to behaviorism implied in the process, or it may be justified by know-nothing scientism, or concerns for efficiency and accountability. It comes to the adoption of some such slogans as 'knowing is doing', or 'understanding is doing'. To know mathematics *is* to be able to do certain sorts of things. Tests require people to do the things they must do if they can be said to know mathematics. If one can do these things one knows mathematics; if one cannot do them one does not know mathematics. We define the quality of someone's knowledge of mathematics by the things he can or cannot do. If we cannot describe some quality of someone's knowledge of mathematics in what he can do, we cannot test for its presence. The philosophical behaviorist might say that we should limit the curriculum in mathematics to those things we can observe people doing because that is all there is to a knowledge of mathematics. Those concerned for efficiency might say there is no point in including anything that cannot be defined in observable performance terms because one could not tell whether anything of the sort was being learned or taught. Those concerned with accountability could say 'If this is what your students should be doing, show us that they are doing it or show us the reasons why they are not.'

Now, some subjects, such as mathematics and its branches, are more systematically described in terms of logical operations or defined elements and assumptions than are a number of other subjects. Indeed, mathematics and the physical sciences might have considerable advantage over art, music, dance, history, and literature when it comes to the specification in behavioral terms of knowledge or understanding or appreciation of these areas. We know when we have been presented with a proper solution to a problem in algebra:

the logic holds or it does not; it meets the specified terms of the problem in accordance with the specified rules of algebra. When it comes to art, what on earth is a solution to a problem, any how? One hears artists and critics use such expressions, but they are rather different from solutions to algebra problems. The logical framework is not there. The judgment of performance in music, art, literary skill, or critical skill is a rather different sort of business from judgment where one can get it right or get it wrong, demonstrably, where hard proof is possible. One can more readily discover whether a child is learning to read and how well he can read and comprehend what the words mean, than whether he reads with sensitivity or is developing a feel for the possibilities of language. There is more agreement on the nature of the evidence for reading and vocabulary development than for literary sensitivity and feeling for the possibilities of language.

The more room that is given to subjects amenable to precision and objectivity in the curriculum, the more efficient the curriculum might be made. Where time is limited and the number of things one might include is large, choices have to be made. What better way than to include first those subjects in which learning can best be measured? This is one way of distinguishing the fundamentals of schooling from the frills.

Oddly enough, behaviorism has become identified with written tests and objectivity of evaluation with a most peculiar result. Performance on the test is 'behavior' and is taken to be more objectively reliable than other forms of behavior. Concern for test objectivity and reliability at the expense of validity have combined to undermine subject integrity. To explain a few terms briefly: objectivity here is meant to convey the idea that the evidence is clear and available to all in the same way — the need for opinion or judgment is minimized in scoring an evaluation, for example; reliability means the extent to which the same sorts of answers are given to the same sorts of questions by the same sorts of people in the same sorts of circumstances; validity means the extent to which the questions evaluate what it is they are intended to evaluate.

It is then possible to have an objective test that yields reliable results and is nonetheless not testing what one wants to test in the first place. The art teacher, the physical education teacher, the music teacher, the woodwork teacher, the dance teacher, the cookery teacher, the literature teacher, the history teacher, want solid objective evaluations of their students. They would reduce the arbitrariness or the subjectivity of their everyday evaluations of student performance as product. They want a measuring device that will provide the same evidence continuously available in the same way to any pair of eyes that might examine it. The written examination which asks questions which have a right and a wrong answer allowing for the minimum in interpretation on the part of those taking it and those scoring it would best fit the bill. If there are interpretations, they had better be the safe or standard interpretations dominant in the field and agreed on by evaluators.

With such examinations in hand all of our teachers can point to the measurable outcomes of their instruction. They are as accountable as the mathematics or physics teacher. Each can claim that his subject's inclusion in the curriculum is no less an efficient use of time and money than any other's. But each has sold his soul in the process.

The tests do not examine what is of greatest significance in each of these subjects. The literature test that seeks factual answers about 'who said what in which novel' or 'who said what about some character' hardly tests literary sensitivity or judgment. The history test that asks for no more than the reproduction of names and dates and the textbook's five causes of the Civil War is a test of memory, albeit a memory of historical knowledge, but no more than that. A test of the rules of tennis, or of the steps 'by the numbers' in hitting a tennis serve properly, hardly does justice to the evaluation of someone's progress in mastering tennis. Exams on cooking procedures are poor substitutes for the evaluation of success in the kitchen. Getting the right answers in an 'honesty' exam indicates only that the student is aware of the answers he is supposed to supply. Whether he believes in them or acts in accordance with them is another matter entirely. Performance on the examination is behavior, but it is not the right behavior — it is not the behavior that one wants to evaluate.

The adoption of such examinations and the concern for objectivity in evaluation are often insidious in their effects on curriculum at the level of what is taught in each subject. If success is to be evaluated and school marks are to be given by grades on these exams, then students who care about succeeding at school and getting high marks will demand greater emphasis in their classwork on preparation for such exams. Teachers who expound about truth and beauty and human judgment, who try to engage students in the exercise of critical judgment, and yet ask on exams only 'who said what to whom' are considered hypocritical and unfair. Students learn to tune out the 'extraneous stuff' and 'swot up the facts' for the exam. Teachers concerned about their reputation for successful teaching, as measured by the success of their students on examinations, feel pressed to concentrate their efforts on preparing their students for exams, especially if these are school wide or nation wide exams, which permit comparative ranking of students by teacher and school. This is a picture of what we have always found wrong with teaching to the exam. The examination deadens the curriculum; the more 'objective' the exam, the more potentially deadening its effects. Behavioral definition of educational objectives only provides a new sense of legitimacy for a long-standing distortion of our educational intentions.

Testing and teaching may become so confused with one another that teaching becomes testing. Behavioral definition does not merely delineate objectives, it may be permitted to dictate teaching practice. If teaching is construed as getting students to know things, if knowledge may be defined as competent performance, if competent performance is defined as scoring at some particular level of correct response to items on an examination, then teaching may take the form of practice in getting things right on examination. The behavioral technologists in educational psychology have given us 'programmed learning', the teaching machine (with or without 'hardware'). The teacher is reduced to machine operator. Learning is reduced to the mechanical process of ingesting bits of information and spewing them back in bits as called for. Even if the program only asks questions, they are so designed ideally as to take the students from what he knows already, in discrete steps, to the answering of questions he could not have answered originally. If he gets stuck at some point, he may be directed to review the steps to that point either by literal repetition or by an alternative equivalent sub-program.

Programmed learning is the technological extension of the old exercise, drill, and quiz form of teaching. Many of us went through a number of school subjects in which all we ever did was to answer exercise questions at home, review the answers in class, drill on the correct responses and take daily quizzes until, at intervals, we would take larger examinations requiring us to remember blocks of what we were to have learned in this daily cumulative fashion. The teacher, especially one following a text and workbook or a set curriculum guide, was as much a machine operator then as under the newer programmed learning. Only the machines are more finely tuned now. The teacher may need to know even less about the subject than earlier. Indeed, one suspects that programmed learning was intended to correct the gaps in efficiency of uninspired and uninformed teaching with the limited methods of exercise, drill, and quiz.

Now, this is not a blanket indictment of either the old or the new machine approach to teaching. Both can be effective, especially in getting students to soak up what they might otherwise have to read or listen to, and remember or figure out. What is indicted is the identification of the approach with teaching. There are two fundamental difficulties with so doing: one is practical and the other is conceptual, though with practical consequences.

On the practical side there is the new version of the old problems of exercise, drill, and quiz. We used to complain about learning being mechanical, superficial, and transitory. Students would go through the motions of doing their exercises, etc. (if they did not merely copy the answers from one another); they might even remember the answers or solutions to exercise problems as asked. They might be able to perform well in drill and quiz. Still, they might have no sense of what they are doing. The questions and answers might have no meaning at all to them. The memory took it all in and spewed it out on cue — in through the eyes and ears and out of the mouth, through the fingers with as little engagement of thinking mind as possible. The object was not to know or understand the material; the object was to get credit for the work and pass the quizzes. Those who could and did exercise their minds might make connections among the things they picked up. Some might even prepare themselves for exams that required the making of connections. Teachers were often afraid to administer such exams for fear that (or because they had good experiential grounds to be sure that) students could not handle them. Where the process involves so little engagement of mind, where it encourages little discussion, where it is permitted to engender little interest beyond the exam, and where students themselves see little use for the knowledge gained, there is little need to retain it for very long.

The very efficiency of modern programmed learning in breaking down knowledge into discrete elements, by-passing depth of thought and discussion, may allow the student to get through a program so painlessly as to retain nothing beyond the examination on it. The premium is on passing the exam; the course consists in passing the exam. The student who views schooling as the game of passing exams and adding up points toward a diploma need have no commitment to learning anything at all. Schooling becomes a charade. Instead of furnishing the mind with knowledge, enhancing intellectual capacity and the development of character, schooling fills the mind with a disconnected hodge podge of half-remembered trivia with little if any practice in making sense of it and reinforces the student in the cynicism of the whole process and readiness to take life as a matter of getting by or getting ahead as best one can. Surely this is the behavioral quest for a science of the improvement of man and society gone wrong.

But it does not just go wrong in practice. Teaching as testing is at bottom a conceptual mistake. More precisely it is a collection of conceptual mistakes. Most fundamentally, knowledge is not to be confused with behavior. Granted, the only way of telling whether someone knows something is by getting him to present evidence of his knowledge. But drilling him in the answers to questions testing knowledge is not getting him to know the subject. Rather it is 'planting the evidence' of knowledge; it is getting him to behave as if he knows the subject. If we were to give the same examination to two students, one who had been drilled on the answers and one who had to figure them out for himself, the identical scores they might turn in would certainly not indicate identical knowledge of the subject. If knowledge were merely behavior, if knowledge of a subject could be broken down into bits as appropriate responses to examination instructions, then there would be no distinction to be made in these two cases. But we want to insist that there is a vast difference in the knowledge of one who knows enough to figure out the appropriate responses and one who can only recognize the cues for a previously learned response. We must be very careful in the way we teach lest we undermine the capacity for knowledge, for understanding, appreciation, the exercise of judgment, in sum what distinguishes the trained animal from the educated human. La Mettrie saw no distinction in the training of the animal and the training of human intellectual achievement. Such was the hope of his science of behavior (1748).

The hope remains, but it is, at bottom, misguided if it is taken too literally as the programming into the individual of specific behavioral responses to the appropriate stimuli. One who knows literature or who understands history may provide his own stimuli for behavior when sheer interest or curiosity leads him to think about relationships among the things he knows. His knowledge could eventuate in a variety of forms. The things he says or writes may be virtual equivalents as indices of his knowledge. An examination of his knowledge in an exhaustive sense eliciting everything he might conceivably be prepared to present as evidence of his knowledge would require omniscience on the part of the examiner, if all the appropriate responses were to be built into the exam. When we talk about one's knowledge with this sense of quality in mind, then we can only talk about an examination that might *sample* one's knowledge of a subject.

And again, we must be careful not to confuse a sample of one's knowledge of a subject with the nature of that knowledge itself. Earlier, I spoke of the confusion of behavior on an examination with behavior in the pursuit of some activity. Examination behavior is not artistic behavior or dancing behavior or woodworking behavior. No amount of so-called operational definition can get around that. The confusion of testing and teaching, particularly of written testing and teaching, in subjects such as these rests on just such a conceptual confusion. It is just this conceptual confusion that infects the new behavioral vogue in the preparation of teachers.

Behaviorism in Teacher Education —
Old Vinegar in New Bottles

The effort to make teacher education more rigorous, scientific or professional (pick your own euphemism) has recently reached a new high (or low) in the development of what is usually abbreviated as C/PBTE.[1] The 'C' stands for Competency (*sic*). The rest stands for Performance Based Teacher Education. Teachers are to demonstrate competence. Competence in what? Competence in teaching performance. The basis for the development of competent teaching performance is in a Performance Based Teacher Education program.

So far so good. After all, we all want competent teachers. We want teachers who can do the job, who can perform. We do not want people who can talk about teaching; we want people who can teach.

If all we do in teacher education is talk at prospective teachers and have them talk back at us, we have not prepared them to perform as teachers. If we are to attest to their competence when they leave our training programs, we must have evidence of their teaching performance. They must have practical experience in the classroom. They need to observe experienced teachers over time in genuine classroom settings. They need to teach as apprentices under experienced master teachers.

Of course if they are to be competent teachers they also need to know other things as well. Psychology, and testing, and curriculum are important to the competent teacher as well as some idea of the nature of educational research. Then there is the subject matter to be taught. Surely competence in teaching requires competence in subject matter. Perhaps one wants teachers to have some breadth in their educational background beyond the narrow demands of vocationalism. One can even demand evidence of competence in the ability to handle basic knowledge in a variety of subjects.

So, what is new in all this? Thus far this sounds very much like the sort of thing that has been going on in teacher education for generations. But, the emphases are changed. The language is the language of behaviorism in schooling. There is a new jargon. There is an explosion in educational paperwork and in the expansion of the bureaucracy to deal with it. And teaching as testing has subverted any reasonable hope of improvement in the quality of teaching or of teachers.

There is a debate of long standing about the relative importance of competence in mastery of subject matter as against the professional preparation of teachers. On the one side are those who jump from the obvious point that what one does not know one cannot teach to the dubious conclusion that all one needs is a knowledge of a subject in order to teach it. On the other side are those who point out the teaching failures among the untrained but knowledgeable, and jump to the conclusion that there is a body of expertise that can turn people into effective teachers. (At times there is even a hint of anti-intellectualism in the unwarranted conclusion that those who are bright and know a lot about their subject areas are somehow unsuited for careers in teaching.) The debate is further complicated by divisions within the notion of professional preparation. Generally, these are: the most practical — classroom observation and apprentice teaching; the middling practical — methods of teaching courses presenting dos and don'ts of lesson planning, testing, grading, etc. in general and in specific subjects; and least (or un) practical — the foundational courses in educational history, philosophy and psychology. In the US people in the academic disciplines generally concede some importance to practice teaching and perhaps some direct instruction in teaching technology. They have reservations about the academic respectability of the educational history, philosophy, and psychology.

Within professional education the lines are drawn between those representing the latter, who often see themselves as intellectually a cut above the practitioners, and the methods people, who have pretentions themselves of a theoretic sort, while the teachers in the classrooms see classroom experience and observation as most central to teacher preparation. Generations of classroom teachers trained in teacher education programs have complained of the abstract irrelevance of the foundation courses, the impracticality of their methods courses, and the lack of direction in their classroom apprenticeship. They complain of a sense of incompetence to perform as teachers when their teacher preparation has been completed.

The central idea in Performance Based Teacher Education is to reconstruct professional education such that everything in it is aimed at making the teacher in training a competent practitioner. If there is no pay-off in performance, there is no justification for inclusion of the component. But how is performance to be judged?

One might suppose that master teachers or supervisors might be prepared to judge the quality of their apprentices. However, as many of those who have represented teacher training programs in the supervision of apprentice teachers can attest, master teachers are extremely hesitant to give low marks to their apprentices. It is difficult to convey in words the sense of frustration that comes when a master teacher confesses privately, or complains to others, about the total unsuitability for teaching of an apprentice and yet this same teacher has turned in passing marks for the apprenticeship. How is the institutional representative to explain his assigning anything less than passing marks in the face of the master teacher's *written* recommendation? Officials of the teacher training institution are hesitant to provide less than passing marks for apprentice teachers in that the apprentice usually enrolls for practice teaching as the culmination of his professional preparation. How can the institution explain its failure to 'counsel such potential incompetents out' of the teacher preparation program. And more than one Dean has told me that this explanation may have to satisfy a judge in court of law should the apprentice teacher enter a suit against the institution. It appears the institution should endeavor to gather evidence of potential teaching competence early on and that there must be evidence of competence or incompetence objective enough to stand up in court.

Academic politics, economic and legal interests aside, it does seem to make good sense that those who think they would like to become teachers should discover as early as they can in their training program whether they are suited to the profession. Before too much is invested, it is useful that those who would bear the cost of their preparation, the family or the state, should discover whether the investment is likely to pay off. To require earlier and greater exposure to the working classroom does not, in and of itself, guarantee any such discovery. Some will decide for themselves that they do not want to teach when they see what teachers have to put up with on a daily basis. Others may be encouraged to pursue other options. If, however, it is left to their teachers in classrooms and training programs to decide on the marks they give, then there is little gained in the added classroom exposure in the way of sorting the desirables from the undesirables. Again the cry goes up for objective criteria by which to evaluate competence and teaching potential.

The most obvious criterion might be a determination of whether classroom pupils learn from the teacher candidate. This raises an extremely sensitive issue. Since the classroom pupils are the responsibility of the regularly assigned teacher, it is embarrassing and potentially legally dangerous to admit that they were permitted to learn less effectively than they might have under the regular teacher. One must also be in a position to determine what learning is clearly attributable to the novice and what to the regular teacher. Where the novice is only a teacher aide in the early stages of training this may be very difficult to determine. Finally, making student learning the index to relative teaching effectiveness constitutes a threat to the regular classroom teacher who is necessarily being evaluated as to effectiveness in the process of rating the novice by comparison.

It is not surprising, then, that the quest for objectivity in evaluation should lead to the call for behavioral definition of teacher education objectives. Given the concern for performance, why not specify the sorts of performance to be expected of a competent teacher? Good teaching may be reduced to the things that a good teacher does. Then one can have teachers in training practice doing those things and one can observe whether they do them and check them off as done. If they are not done then one can note the absence of checks. The trouble is that there is not very clear agreement on just what it is that good teachers do that distinguishes them from mediocre or bad teachers.

We know what is not good teaching, minimally. If one cannot control a classroom of students, one cannot teach them anything. If one misinforms a class, one miseducates them. If one cannot keep to the subject for very long, or is incoherent, one cannot present a coherent picture of the subject. Nevertheless, one cannot present a list of discrete positive behaviors that constitute a recipe for good teaching.

Unless teaching is construed as 'tending a teaching machine' or merely running children through the routines provided to the teacher in a mechanical fashion, teaching is an intellectually demanding business. Teachers may have all sorts of routine at their fingertips, they may have all sorts of classroom management or crisis management or individual motivational ploys available. Good teaching is a matter of knowing when to use which with whom. It is a matter of judgment, of day-to-day alertness to cues, trial and error to know that Jane needs stern treatment today and Johnny needs encouragement. It is a good teacher, indeed, who can capitalize on the creativity of a pupil's wrong answer to a question and realize *that* the student was thinking and *what* the student was thinking. Such a teacher must understand very well what it means to think in the subject in order to correct the pupil's thinking in that subject.

Now, one might object that this *is* a description, or at least a partial description, of good teaching in behavioral terms. Of course it is. If we could not describe what a good teacher does, how would we know one when we saw one? In teacher education, as in any kind of schooling, we must have evidence, we must observe behavior to determine what the individual can do. The problem is not merely to list what good teachers do. The problem is to decide what it is to have novices do to become good teachers. We cannot simply say 'Recognize a good insightful wrong answer.' Either the novice can do it or not. Just as with behavioral definition in general, a set of specifications as to the qualities of the product do not define the process by which to turn out that product.

We can at least see to it that the novice has some experience in doing the various sorts of things that we expect teachers to do. We can set up a check list of professional behaviors: administer and score various sorts of standardized tests (list), operate various sorts of audiovisual equipment (list), write and administer own teacher made test, write lesson plans of various types, write questionnaires and plot sociograms, give a classroom presentation with filmstrip, etc. We can call these teacher behaviors and we can attest to the novice's familiarity with and, to some extent, competence in each of these things. But, the novice might be checked out on all of these things as competent and still not be a very competent teacher. The novice might not be able to put it all together and teach. He might come to the apprentice teaching experience and fizzle out in confusion or ineptitude. We might be able to specify the contents of the behavioral repertoire of the teacher and yet be unable to ensure their intelligent utilization in teaching. Teaching is like a craft; it is more than the sum total of the worker's skills. It requires a sense of fittingness in the application of tools to materials for specific purposes appropriate both to the materials and to the artist's intentions. We can describe the doing of it when it is done, but we cannot program it in advance for all teachers and students. Unfortunately, those things that we can ask teachers in training to do and check off our list as done become the core of evidence, the behavioral evidence of competence in Performance Based Teacher Education.

Equally unfortunate is the tendency to seek behavioral evidence of competence in all aspects of the teacher education program. Some states in the United States require institutions that train teachers to specify their objectives in behavioral terms. Somehow each sub-course of instruction in each of the subject areas in the professional training sequence and in those arts and sciences, the study of which is expected of teachers, must be described in terms of purposes, goals, and objectives (as though a recognized distinction exists among the three). Instructors are required to list the behavioral objectives, heads of departments are required to compile such lists for further compilation by Deans of schools of education for presentation to state departments of education so that the content of the teacher training programs may be evaluated. It is as though education, the education of the teacher could be reduced to a set of engineer's specifications. The quality of what is taught and how it is taught is hardly captured in such specification. The quality of student performance may vary widely from one training institution to another in meeting nominally similar behavioral objectives. There are no defined or enforced uniformities of standard. Compliance with the state's demands easily degenerates into a ritualism where a few people sit down with lists of preferred objectives as published by some such agency as the National Association of State Directors of Teacher Education and Certification (1973) (there really is such an agency and such lists) or as published by the state (Pigge, 1978) and they copy them off to save everyone else the time and trouble of working them out. The result is an expanded bureaucracy at teacher training institutions and in state departments of education whose primary functions are to feed and feed on piles of paper that have no useful bearing on the quality of instruction in the training or education of teachers. It is a waste of money to support such an enterprise; it is demeaning to the profession of teaching at *all* levels to have to engage in such empty ritualism.

The emptiness of the ritual is best exemplified in the infighting among the representatives of the various components of professional preparation for inclusion in the new teacher training. The foundations of education and methods people are not about to go out of business. If they cannot show direct application of their offerings to performance in the classroom, performance must be reconstrued to include the measurable student outcomes of their instruction whatever that might be. Knowledge of philosophy of education is construed as performance on an examination on philosophy of education. If it is performance, it fits in Performance Based Teacher Education. If the performance can be scored then there is an objective measure of competence in performance.[2]

The final absurdity comes with the idea that teacher candidates who can demonstrate competence in meeting behavioral objectives in the teacher education program may proceed through the program in due course. Why absurd? Competence in performance may even be defined as attainment of a set score in a written examination or in the doing of a set of assignments on a check list. Courses of study in professional education may be reduced to the contents of examinations in the same way as subjects in the curriculum were described as reduced earlier on. And of course academic areas required of teachers may be similarly reduced. The curriculum of teacher education is confused with the testing of knowledge and, with self-pacing programmed instruction, teaching teachers is thoroughly confused with testing.

Examination performance is not teaching performance. Competence in examination performance is not competence in teaching performance. The expansion of the notion of performance to include examination performance permits the inclusion in C/PBTE of everything and anything included in teacher education before its adoption. The confusion of teaching and testing does not enhance the professional status and quality of teacher training but reduces teacher training and schooling and education in general to rote and ritual. We would do well to give up the language and ritual of this monstrous sort of educational behaviorism. And yet we should not forget the essential truth — we are committed to behaviorism in schooling. If we would have people learn and improve the process, we must do things, they must do things and we must try to evaluate what we do and they do. But let us not confuse these very different things. If we want people to develop their powers of judgment and discrimination, we must give them opportunities to exercise judgment and discrimination. We cannot program these things into them by the numbers. And there are some things that we deem so important, as in character development for example, that we must try to develop them even though the results of our efforts cannot always be assessed while our pupils are in school. Behaviorism in schooling is not a device for making of the young what we will. Nor is it the instrument for remaking a society as we would wish.

NOTES

1. The American Association of Colleges for Teacher Education has been publishing occasional papers and reports about and on behalf of Performance Based Teacher Education, under the auspices of the PBTE project.
2. An official of a state department of education made just such a representation to me.

CHAPTER 5

Behaviorism and the
Idea of Control

There is yet another concern about behaviorism in general and
behaviorism in schooling in particular. Like other such concerns,
this one rests on confusions between behavioral science and
behavioral engineering. This sort of confusion may be built in
behaviorism, as noted earlier, in the optimism of those who would
advance the study of behavior in order to learn how to enhance the
state of man and civilization. At any rate, the scientific nature of
control is confused with the ordinary notions of power — power to
shape man's mind and destiny, power to manipulate man's behavior,
power to rule over man politically. The purity and nobility of the
scientific quest for knowledge is attributed by some people to the
motivations of the scientists engaged in that quest. Who but such
pure and noble scientists should be entitled to the power of creating
and managing an ideal society? Where benevolence and expertise are
supposed to be assured, who could oppose a benevolent despotism of
experts? On the other hand, there are some who automatically
suspect the character of those who might assume such power. 'Power
tends to corrupt; absolute power corrupts absolutely,' said Lord
Acton (1887). The issue is moot. The power is not there or what there
is is scarcely absolute. It is not that a despot could not rule with
absolute power. Rather behaviorism as science or as technology and
especially behaviorism in schooling do not have or confer on anyone
the power to do all the things hoped for or feared.

In science one controls variables, not people. If one is to isolate the
effect or importance of one variable, say parent's education, on the
value of another variable, say school achievement, one wants to be

sure that other variables are controlled. Suppose we found that the greater the number of years of parental schooling, the higher the level of the educational achievement of their offspring. We might jump to the conclusion that increasing the years of schooling in one generation would increase the educational achievement of the next. But perhaps there are other variables operating here. Suppose those parents with the longer number of years of education are better endowed intellectually, or better placed socially, or culturally or economically advantaged or were more highly inculcated by their parents with the idea of the importance of education and have similarly inculcated their children. And suppose they choose to live among similarly affluent, advantaged, endowed or motivating parents such that the school environment of their children is geared toward the promotion of educational achievement among those who come to school ready, able, and willing to strive for achievement. Suppose parental education in the absence of some of these factors, say cultural milieu and living patterns, was not so likely to be followed by offspring achievement. These variables must be controlled in some fashion to replace all the 'supposes' with the values of the variables, with proportions, with estimates of the extent to which each of the variables enters into the originally observed findings. When the variables are thus *controlled* or *understood* or *accounted for,* the simple conclusion that increased years of parental schooling causes increased school achievement of offspring may turn out to have been a simple minded conclusion.

As the scientist improves his ability to account for the relative influence of variables as they have affected some process or outcome, he may talk about predictive control of the process or outcome. Those things that have made a difference in the past are assumed to make a difference in the future. The extent to which they appear to have made a difference is converted into a set of probabilities that they will continue to make a difference in the future. Where past associations duly measured and controlled are high, predictive probabilities are also high. And some of the more robust scientists might talk about predictive control approaching virtual certainty.

Now, in the example of the relationship of level of parental education and school achievement of their children, I jumped fairly early to a conclusion, as though I had predictive control. It came down to a policy to improve school achievement in the next generation through the provision or compulsion of longer school attendance for

Behaviorism and Schooling

the members of the present generation. It is as though the purported predictive control told us what to do. If we had the power to control school attendance now, we would have the power to bring about a school achievement later. Notice how predictive control slides so readily into control as power to manipulate. Perhaps this is where the old saw comes from that 'knowledge is power'. To know what is the cause of a desired effect is to know where to intervene to *supply* the cause to bring about the effect.

Note as well that, in the case at hand, increased scientific control might just as well document the influence of causes over which we have no power. Predictive control might tell us that bright parents raise bright children to be bright parents, that those who have been motivated enough to seek extended education try to see to it that their children are similarly motivated, that those who come from certain sorts of home environments in particular sorts of cultural back-grounds instill a proper sense of motivation toward educational achievement in generation after generation. We might be able to predict with virtual certainty those who are most likely to do well in school and yet be relatively powerless to intervene in the lives of the mass of mankind to influence their educational achievement. We could have excellent scientific control and, in practice, no control. Sometimes knowledge confers power and sometimes it merely documents our impotence.

Perhaps, though, this impotence may be overcome. There is a sense in which the social scientist becomes a behavioral engineer because he is prepared to take drastic action to reform or reconstruct society (with or without the trauma of political revolution). The notion of engineer is broadened with the expansion of the scope of his purview to the society at large and the operation of a society's institutions. The basic model is no longer that of behavioral psychology seeking laws and mechanisms by which behavior is created, shaped, and modified. Rather, the approach is more holistic. This raises the issue of methodological individualism versus holism in social science and social engineering.[1]

The Social Engineer vs the Behavioral Mechanic

In the example of parents and the educational attainment of their offspring there was very little mention of the *mechanisms* by which parents or others directly influenced that achievement. Predictive control consisted in the accounting (statistical) for achievement by reference to various characteristics of parents and environment. I did not say *how* parents motivated their children to achieve in school; I said *that* parents of certain cultural backgrounds did this. Indeed, a researcher might infer this from the fact that people of certain cultural backgrounds were motivated to educational achievement generation after generation. The researcher assumes, perhaps by eliminating other variables, that there *must* have been something those parents were doing to motivate their children. One might be quite sure on the basis of evidence that an environment in which the children of such parents are brought together in relative isolation from others in society would be conducive to the reinforcement of motivation for school achievement. Now, this is not to say that there are no particular practices or mechanisms of parental motivation or mechanisms of environmental reinforcement of attitudes and even of improvement of educational attainment. What it does say is that one may have excellent scientific or predictive control of a relatively holistic sort. One need not know *how* something comes about in order to know *under what conditions, for what people,* or *under what institutional arrangements it will come about.* One can make large scale predictions about the shape of society and its direction without invoking either mysterious forces in history or reducing social science to the study of the mechanisms by which individuals are influenced by culture or by which individuals influence culture.

One can predict what large numbers of people are likely to do without necessarily knowing what any given individual is likely to do. If I am assigning automobile insurance policy fees, I do not need to know *why* it is the case that young males have had a higher accident rate than other identifiable age and sex groups; it is a good bet that, as a group, they are likely to have more accidents. Not all members of this group will have accidents and some will have 'more than their share'. I need not know much about why people have automobile accidents to know that there will be very few in those countries that have few automobiles or that there will be relatively few on the Sabbath day in certain countries in which the institution of religion is strong and part of the religion involves strict observance of the Sabbath. Whether the behavior is enforced by law or custom, and how, may interest some, but the predictability of the finding might not be enhanced by the addition of this information.

Now, institutions and social group practices and characteristics often describe behavior in various ways and more or less directly. Social institutions are the accepted (whether officially in doctrine or unofficially in practice) means for carrying out particular sorts of culturally defined activity. There are religious, economic, political, etc. institutions of a society that define what are the usual or accepted ways of engaging in the practice of religion, the business of making a living, the process of ordering the life of society. Characteristics of groups and types of people are often the description of the characteristic ways in which people of certain sorts act in certain circumstances. We might characterize a group as aggressive, or peace loving, as ambitious, hardworking, as honest, as fun loving, etc. The members tend to behave in certain ways. Conceivably, then, one could call the business of prediction by relation to institutions and some characteristics a form of behavioral prediction. But remember that this is stretching the idea as compared to the notion described earlier of predicting and explaining in terms of the mechanism of behavioral influence.

There is an even greater strain on the idea when we note that some characteristics are not readily definable as behavior at all. A young adult male just *is* someone of *a sort*. He is not of that sort because of what he does. The classification is biological and chronological not behavioral. To describe and to predict the behavior of young adult males by virtue of their being young adults who are male is not to explain or predict behavior by reference to behavior. We might also classify groups by reference to beliefs. In some cases the beliefs may be beliefs about how one ought to behave, what one ought to do and ought not to do. Beliefs (professed) about behavior may relate very highly with actual behavior, but the beliefs are not themselves behavior. Moreover, some beliefs, as in belief in ghosts or in gods or in materialism or in extrasensory perception, might correlate very highly with particular sorts of behavior or social institutions (whether higher incidence of suicide, or sexual taboos or whatever), even though the beliefs themselves do not describe what one does or ought to do at all, let alone in the predicted fashion. Imagine high predictive control in this way between a set of beliefs and tendencies to behave in certain ways where the behavior appears to have nothing to do with the specific beliefs in question. Surely there is no sense at all in confusing control of the scientist and manipulative control. There is no mechanism laid bare here with which the social engineer might tinker. Or so it would seem.

Suppose the social engineer were to be concerned to improve society by eliminating the operation of social class bias and racial prejudice. More specifically, suppose he wished to eliminate the unfair effects of such bias and prejudice on the distribution of opportunities for participation in those occupations and activities providing the greater satisfaction in material, spiritual, and intellectual achievement. If he is a heavy-handed sort of reformer, he might try to enforce a lottery system for material reward or a policy approaching 'From each according to his ability, to each according to his need' and mount a propaganda campaign about the 'satisfaction of trash collecting well-done is on a par with neurosurgery or virtuoso violin performance'. Worse yet, he might interchange the trash-collector and the neurosurgeon (not precisely what the Chinese cultural revolution fell into, but not far off the mark).

The trouble with this sort of social engineering is that it just does not appear to work very well in practice. People's attitudes towards rewards as incentives to work and as providing meaning to work are not so easily manipulated. Neurosurgeons make better trash-collectors than trash-collectors make neurosurgeons. Where a society needs specialists with trained talent, it must provide incentives to encourage them to make the sacrifice of long training to see the specialty as conferring special meaning to their lives as they are representatives of a small class of those qualified for its practice. The very need for specialists who can do what most cannot do introduces consideration of personal worth and status. 'Everyone may be beautiful in his own way' as we used to say, but some forms of beauty are more rare than others.

The social engineer might recommend, as indicated, the effort to influence beliefs of people and he might recommend the reconstruction of social and economic institutions in such a way as to effect the changes in the proposed direction. If he has access to the seats of power, his ideas might be translated into action. And, as indicated, they might be met with frustration. If that should happen, he should be expected, as a good empiricist engineer, to recognize his failure, to seek out the 'bugs' in his proposals, or to abandon them and try something else. He may seek to discover further characteristics about the institutions with which he is dealing or of the people whom he would change; he may look to the mechanisms of institutional change and the implantation of beliefs or some combination of the two. He may find, for example, that his ideal of equal material reward for all work does not seem consistent with a consumer goods distribution system based on pricing in accordance with demand for particular goods and scarcity of supply. Perhaps he has not done a thorough enough job of altering the economic institutions. If consumer prices vary with cost of production, how is it that labor prices are not to vary with cost of producing (training, preparing, educating) the labor? The people in some parts of the country may be more amenable to proposed changes than in others; there may be age and sex differences in willingness to adopt the new beliefs and social practices. There may be differences in educational background. There may be beliefs about the need for status ascription in the arrangement of social affairs among more tradition-bound segments of society — not in continuing the status of given occupations, necessarily, but that some status differentiation is necessary to such things as arrangement of marriages and the selection of leaders and magistrates at the local political level. Such beliefs may pervade what is essentially an interlocking network of institutions tying together all segments of life. It might occur to the social engineer that the entire structure of society must be replaced.

Now, this is the nightmare of the political liberal. Examples of such large scale social engineering that come to mind might be Nazi Germany, Soviet Russia of the 1920s and 1930s, Communist China in the time of the Red Guard. The lives and interests of people are too sacred to permit the tampering of social engineers in their experimentation on the way to some holistic vision of an ideal, well-constructed society. It is not always clear whether the anti-holistic approach to social science stems from the desire to protect individuals from the excesses and pretentions of utopian social planners and rebuilders or instead that the hostility to utopianism comes from the view that a holistic social science is *necessarily* pretentious.

There is some confusion here between ideology and social science that needs to be cleared up. A holistic approach to social science does not require that everything be seen in its entirety as a full blown comprehensive network of beliefs, institutions, and practices. Holism, as a methodological position, a way of doing social science, may take the position that society is to be understood in this way, ultimately, that pieces remain to be filled in, that as in any science the last word may never be in, that tomorrow may bring another angle from which to view the larger picture, if not another piece of the picture to be viewed. The social engineer like the social scientist might only seek the opportunity to inform the management of the social enterprise through the careful monitoring of its progress and in accordance with the reality of success or failure in that progress. The social engineer might be an advisor to any sort of society — democratic (people's or otherwise), or fascistic, or totalitarian (of whatever sort). He is then a sort of consulting engineer. As such he has *no* direct power to control anything in the social sphere. On the other hand, the social engineer might be called upon to run things and then social engineering becomes the corporate state or fascism or totalitarianism of one form or another. It becomes a political ideology when it is advanced as the best way to run things. It is essentially the doctrine that someone who knows what he is about ought to be in charge of society. That someone ought to be able to see the connections among social practices and beliefs and rearrange them in such a way that society remains viable and robust. From their different views of society and knowledge both Plato and B. F. Skinner would have agreed that those qualified to seek knowledge should run society. This view requires not that the ruler/social engineer should know everything in advance but that he be fitted to know and to seek to know as he rules/plans to meet the exigencies that confront him. One cannot complain in opposition that this requires omniscience, because it does not. It does require considerable intelligence, expertise, education, experience and commitment to the interest of society at large — and much more so than can be found or expected in the populace at large.

Individualism, political/social as well as methodological, takes the position that society is no more than its members (though Rousseau waffled on this issue[2]). As a political ideology it views the state or society as necessary to the well-being of its members — as a device for protecting their individual interests from encroaching haphazardly on one another and for the organization of their joint protection from outside attack. The emphasis is upon the control and adjustment of behavior of individuals, in light of the effect of their behavior on individuals. Where social policy is adopted to control or alter behavior it is to be evaluated, subsequently, by its effects on the behavioral options — the freedom and well-being — of the people in society. Whereas the holistic outlook is concerned with movement toward some sort of ideal social structure and planning for it, the individualist outlook is much more concerned with the specific day-to-day impact of the activities of people on one another. What is good for society is some sort of aggregate of what individuals deem good for themselves. The ideal is the protection of the options of the individual consistent with the like protection of the options of all others.

Methodological individualism in the study of society, in social science, is the position that the course of human events is to be understood through the examination of the behavior of individuals impinging on one another and on their social and physical environment. It is concerned with the development and testing of the laws of human behavior. It focuses on the mechanisms by which behavior is modified, or influenced, or affected. It is not concerned with the mere correlations of human characteristics with human behavior, with the mere correlations of beliefs with specific human activities no matter how irrelevant to them those beliefs might be. The concern is not only for gross predictive control, but to account for the process of influence in its workings. As engineer, the methodological individualist is the behavioral technologist type.

Now at first blush it might seem that the political individualist might find the behavioral technologist more congenial than the holist-type social engineer. The technologist deals in particular activity in terms of its particulars. The sort of fine tuning of social policy requiring a sensitivity to effects on individuals of changes as they are made would seem to need just that approach.

However, the holist as engineer is in a sense himself a behaviorist, and he would do well to employ behavioral engineers who deal in particulars as well. In the first place, the holist who concentrates on the adjustment of institutional arrangements and practice — the rules of the social game — is concerned with redefining permissible behavior. He is the sort of behaviorist who focuses on the context of behavior. Even he, as well as the holist concerned with beliefs and attitudes, may be concerned as social engineer with the business of changing attitudes and beliefs and getting people to adopt new social institutions, practices and policies. The holist social engineer in charge of society might be most happy to employ behavioral engineers to implement the putting in place, maintenance and fine tuning of some new social structure. Holism as social *science* need not be involved with methodological individualism. These are just two different ways to study society. Holism as social engineering may be very much involved with methodological individualism for the implementation of policies of social change.

Insofar as holism as social engineering describes the context that is to support the desired social behavior and advocates the creation of that context, holism may be a form of behaviorism. It may be a form of behaviorism with respect to the setting of objectives for society. If institutions are a society's way of doing things, if social ideals involve having people believe certain things about how they should behave toward one another and having people behave in those ways toward one another, then the holist social engineer may be said to be in the business of defining society's objectives in behavioral terms. And that is what frightens people.

Science and Humanism

There is some point to the humanistic antagonism to social engineering and its attendant hostility to behaviorism. The holist social engineer decides what would likely be good for people to believe to support particular forms of desirable behavior. The behavioral mechanic then provides the means for inculcating the belief and/or the behavior to be associated with it. The social engineer and the behaviorial mechanic are seen as working hand in glove. On the one hand people are afraid that the behaviorists will be able to control our lives — the horrors of thought control where someone else determines what we are to think. What if some monster (like a Hitler) were at the controls? Think of the vicious thoughts, the detestable acts we might commit in the name of some monster's ideal. The engineers are given credit for 'scientific know-how', for the ability to do the job.

On the other hand, people are afraid that behaviorists will be given credit for such ability, when in fact they do not have the requisite know-how to do a good enough job. Shallowness of vision and inadequacy of technological capability could give us a society impoverished in culture rather than enriched — a drab society of drab people. Or worse, with such engineers in control it could give us a society in chaos, with institutions that do not work, that are at odds with one another, where the beliefs and aspirations promoted officially are in contradiction with the opportunities built into the social structure.

Ten years ago we went to the moon. Science gave us the technology to do anything we wanted. Or so we thought. We could conquer the oceans with huge super tankers to transport oil. We understood the atom and we could harness its energy to generate electric power plants. We could invent the means to fight noble wars in far off places with less sacrifice of men under arms and with more new equipment fashioned from the spin-offs of modern science adapted to space age technology. And we had oil spills and some delays and then mishaps in nuclear power plants. *Men and equipment* were buried in the sink-hole of a war in South East Asia. Perhaps we were not so clever as we had thought. The men in control of policy did not have to be evil monsters if they tried to implement policy based on technology in the process of development. Playing with matches is dangerous. Someone can get hurt. Playing with nuclear energy could be disastrous. All of us could get hurt. If we were too enthusiastic in our optimism ten years ago as we entered the 'new scientific age', we are probably a bit too strident in our pessimism today. Those who design and manage nuclear power plants are not quite playing around with atomic matches. Still, given the experimental nature of science and technology, they cannot know with utmost certainty precisely what will occur as they advance technology in the future. And, however good the science, however ingenious the technology, it always seems that there is something that can go wrong in their utilization by human beings. One can improve the technical capability for dealing with the physical world. But improving the human capacity to utilize that capability is yet another matter.

Why should optimism be any more justified in behavioral science than in natural science, in social and behavioral engineering any more than in the other engineering fields? Economists as scientists had been telling us for years that one does not have high unemployment, inflation and recession all at the same time. They appear to have advanced from their early confusion at this turn of events by naming it 'stagflation' and, putting on their technologist hats, trying to figure out how to live with it. If the blame falls on the mistakes of political leaders in trying to pursue too many objectives at once (in the US the war on poverty, the war in Vietnam, the space program, etc.) all the more reason to be cautious. There is little to suggest that we have improved very much in our capacity to ensure wisdom on the part of our leaders or the mass of the people.

There is little point, however, in a blanket condemnation of science or technology. We might romanticize about the good old days, when people did not have to worry about oil spills and nuclear disaster. But there were wars that covered continents, diseases that ravaged millions, conflagrations that destroyed whole cities, over the whole course of history. The poor today in most developed countries would have seemed well off by the standards of a century ago or two or three. For most people, life was shorter, harder and devoted more to mere physical survival than anything else.

In fact we have improved the material quality of life considerably. These improvements have been made possible by advances in and understanding of natural forces, by the advancement of natural science and the development of technology. They have also been made possible by improvements in our understanding of human society and advancements in the technology of organization of human activity. The industrial revolution is as much a revolution in the physical response to the physical universe as it is in the social response to the social universe of organizing people for productive work, for the redesign of the institutions of distribution and consumption.

Societies do not freeze in some sort of ideal condition. As Plato foresaw, this world is a world of change. We are always in the middle of things. There are always emergencies to be met, there is always the unfinished business of improving our capacity to deal with illness, disease, hunger, of improving the inclusiveness of our efforts to reduce poverty and its effects. People have new ideas and interests and they pursue them in the development of products, the arts or leisure activities. The pursuit of some interests results in advantage to some people and disadvantage to others. Some interests may be dangerous to the people who pursue them, drugs for example, or the danger may be more widespread, drinking and driving for example. The automobile as ambulance saves countless lives that would otherwise have been lost. The automobile with a drunken driver at the wheel takes lives before their time.

Science is neutral with respect to the reasons people have for its pursuit. That is the ideal of science: to seek to know what is the case, to understand nature on its terms as things are without being influenced by how we would have them be. Technology is neutral with respect to the good or evil intention, the wisdom or folly of its utilization. The fact that technology may be utilized for ignoble ends or may be pursued unwisely does not alter the fact that the advancement of noble ends requires increased knowledge and improvement of our technological capabilities to deal with the world. Whether these requirements can be met and, if so, in timely fashion cannot be guaranteed in advance. There are grounds neither for blind fear nor blind faith in science and technology. There is a sort of faith in science that in itself is blinding. It is called scientism.

Scientism. Common Sense and Sensibility

Scientism comes in two main forms. The first form of scientism consists in the presumption that all problems of life in human society may be cast as scientific and technological problems. The very idea that the social engineer might determine what people ought to think or feel or believe in order to support the institutions and practices that the social engineer determines are good for them, if they think or feel or believe properly about what is good for them, this is scientism run rampant. It is the arrogation by science and technology, or the abrogation to science and technology, of the rights and responsibilities of people to think their own thoughts and to live a life of choice and to work out their priorities among one another. It presumes to answer the questions of philosophy by *fiat* and to eliminate politics as the enterprise of social accommodation. Human society is likened to a factory in need of efficient management. But it is a factory with no other product than its own efficient operation. This view of society is dehumanizing. This idea of efficiency of operation for its own sake is meaningless. This sort of scientism is abhorrent to common sense and to human sensibility.

The other sort of scientism involves the utilization of the mere trappings of science and technology for persuasive purposes. In the earlier discussion of behaviorism in schooling, I pointed out that whatever we were doing in schools, whatever we wished to teach, could be described in the language of behavioral definition of educational objectives. I showed that the advancement of the technology of teaching did not need much if anything from psychology as science or psychology as technology. The stating of educational objectives in the jargon of behavioral psychology does not in itself make them any clearer, nor does it make them any more desirable than before. To present as science what is only a ritual translation of our nice ambiguous objectives, and to pretend to the scientific selection of objectives thereby, is an insult to common sense and an affront to human sensibility. We should not have to put up with such scientism. We should not be impressed by it.

Nor should we forget when we are presented with a whole string of behaviorally defined objectives, that objectives and technology are not quite the same. The social engineer might define the behavioral objectives of a society. He needs the behavioral mechanic to figure out how to attain these objectives. There is an overemphasis in behaviorism in schooling on the setting of objectives in behavioral terms and a rather shallow conception of the behavioral technology necessary to achieve these objectives. Behaviorism in schooling fairly reeks of scientism, the ritual pretense of scientific and technological sophistication.

Now, if such behaviorism in schooling is so much a sham, then schooling as behaviorism is an even worse pretense. It is absurd to suppose that the schools are the instrument for the correction of society's ills, for the fine tuning of the working of society's institutions, through the systematic preparation of the young to man these institutions with a will, with the proper will. We can throw all the objectives we want at the schools, in the most behavioral language we might find. That will not give the schools the control over the young, the power to determine their thoughts and wishes, hopes and ideals, feelings and urges, beliefs and ideas. Students in school are not isolated or insulated from other influences in society. Schools do not monopolize ideas. Just because we wish that the schools could produce ideal citizens in an efficient manner does not give us the right to assume that they can.

And I am not sure that we should encourage school people to try. For, then, someone will have to define just what we mean by ideal citizen. The definition must be specific and yet not so ideal as to require him to be all wise, all loving, all talented, etc. It must be specific, or there is nothing in particular to try to produce. It must not be so ideal as to be impossible of attainment. Presumably we do not wish the schools to produce only one or two ideal citizens out of the mass of students. Either we shall have to find some least common denominator of attributes or some set of virtual equivalent attributes (equivalent virtues?). Are the schools to determine what those shall be or who shall be schooled in what? Are we to determine these for the schools? Who are *we*? Just how systematic do we want the schools to be, assuming the schools could deliver the goods? Are we to fall into the first sort of scientism in which the schools are asked to shape the young as both the materials and the laborers in the society whose end is its managed efficiency?

The alternative is not the world as a madhouse with no one in charge. We are committed politically, philosophically, or spiritually to the democratic ideal that all of us are in charge, and consequently no one of us is in charge. Leadership and the running of the affairs of society are in the hands of those we elect or appoint, only for so long as we elect or appoint them and only for limited purposes. The more diverse we are as a society, the more pluralistic our cultural heritage, attitudes, life-styles, aspirations, the greater the need for tolerance of continued diversity of outlook. Democracy of this sort requires respect for the rights of individuals and groups of individuals to think their own thoughts. It requires individuals of intelligence and ability to serve as leaders. It requires citizens who can recognize such people and promote them to positions of leadership. It requires people who can see the connection between self-interest and contribution to society and shape self-interest in the light of obligation to society.

We may hope and try in schools to prepare our young to understand these things and to value them as we do. And yet we do not all see them or value them in precisely the same way. Our objectives cannot be specified clearly, given our different perceptions of what they mean. The schools cannot be the agency for the fine tuning of a society that does not agree on matters of fine tuning. Where there is no specifiable product there is no intelligible technology for its production. The scientism of behaviorism in schooling and of schooling as behaviorism is a misrepresentation of behaviorism as either science or technology. And it is a misrepresentation of the function of the institution of schooling in a democratic society.

NOTES

1.   There is an excellent discussion of the philosophical issues in methodological

individualism versus holism in Brodbeck (1968) Section 4. See especially articles by Gelner, Watkins and Brodbeck.
2. Especially in the *Social Contract* in discussion of the obligations of the citizen and of the General Will.

Bibliography

ACTON, LORD (John Emerich Dalberg) (1887) letter to Bishop Mandell Creighton.

AMERICAN ASSOCIATION OF COLLEGES FOR TEACHER EDUCATION, PBTE Project, occasional papers on Performance Based Teacher Education (Washington, D.C.).

BERLIN, I. (ed.) (1956) *The Age of Enlightenment; the 18th Century Philosophers* (New York: Mentor Books).

BLOOM, B. S. *et al.* (1956) *Taxonomy of Educational Objectives: The Classification of Educational Goals: Handbook I: Cognitive Domain* (New York: David McKay Co.).

BROADHURST, P. L. (1968) WATSON, JOHN B. *The International Encyclopedia of the Social Sciences* Vol. 16 (New York: Macmillan).

BRODBECK, M. (ed.) (1968) *Readings in the Philosophy of the Social Sciences* (New York: Macmillan).

BUCHLER, J. (1955) *Philosophical Writings of Peirce* (New York: Dover).

CHARLESWORTH, J. C. (1962) (ed.) *The Limits of Behavioralism in Political Science* (Philadelphia: The American Academy of Political and Social Science).

CREMIN, L. (1961) *The Transformation of the School; Progressivism in American Education, 1876-1957* (New York: Alfred A. Knopf).

DEWEY, J. (1899) *The School and Society* (Chicago: The University of Chicago Press).

DEWEY, J. (1916) *Democracy and Education* (New York: Macmillan).

HOFSTADTER, R. (1945) *Social Darwinism in American Thought; 1860-1915* (Philadelphia: University of Pennsylvania).

HUMPHREYS, L. G. (1968) Factor analysis. In *The International Encyclopedia of the Social Sciences* Vol. 5 (New York: Macmillan).

JONCICH, G. M. (ed.) (1962) *Psychology and the Science of Education; Selected Writings of Edward L. Thorndike* (New York: Teachers College, Columbia University).

121

KLEINMUNTZ, B. (ed .) (1966) *Problem Solving: Research, Method and Theory* (New York: Wiley).

LENZER, G. (1975) *Auguste Comte and Positivism; the Essential Writings* (New York: Harper and Row).
LA METTRIE, J. O. de (1748) *Man a Machine.* Philosophical and Historical Notes by G. C. Bussey, (Chicago: The Open Court, 1912).

National Association of State Directors of Teacher Education and Certification (1973) *Standards for State Approval of Teacher Education* (revised ; Washington, D.C.).

PEIRCE, C. S. (1955) The essentials of pragmatism, and Pragmatism in retrospect: a last formulation. In Buchler.
PETERS, R. S. (1959) *Authority, Responsibility and Education* (London: George Allen and Unwin).
PIGGE, F. L. (1978) *An Approach to Program Product Evaluation in Teacher Education* (Columbus: Ohio Department of Education).
PLATO, *Meno.* Trans. B. Jowett, with Introduction by F. H. Anderson, (New York: The Liberal Arts Press, 1949).
PLATO, *The Republic.* Trans. with Introduction and Notes by F. M. Cornford (London: Oxford University Press, 1941).
POTTS, D. C. and CHARLTON, D. G. (1972) *French Thought Since 1600* (London: Methuen).

ROSENTHAL, R. and JACOBSON, L. (1968) *Pygmalion in the Classroom* (New York: Holt, Rinehart and Winston).
ROUSSEAU, JEAN JACQUES *Emile.* Trans. B. Foxley, with Introduction by A. B. DeMonvel (London: J. M. Dent, 1957).
ROUSSEAU, JEAN JACQUES, *The Social Contract.* Introduction by C. Frankel (New York: Hafner, 1947).
RYLE, G. (1949) *The Concept of Mind* (New York: Barnes and Noble).

SCHEFFLER, I. (1974) *Four Pragmatists, A Critical Introduction to Peirce, James, Mead and Dewey* (Atlantic Highlands: Humanities Press).
SCHULTZ, T. W. (1971) *Investment in Human Capital: the Role of Education and of Research* (New York: The Free Press).
SKINNER, B. F. (1948) *Walden Two* (New York: Macmillan).
SKINNER, B. F. (1971) *Beyond Freedom and Dignity* (New York: Alfred A. Knopf).
SPENGLER, O. (1926) *The Decline of the West.* Trans. C. F. Atkinson (London: George Allen and Unwin).

THORESEN, C. E. (ed .) (1973) *Behavior Modification in Education.* The National Society for the Study of Education (Chicago: the University of Chicago Press).

THORNDIKE, R. L. (1969) Review of *Pygmalion in the Classroom. Teachers College Record,* Vol. 70, No. 8, May.

WEBER, M. (1949) *The Methodology of the Social Sciences* (New York: The Free Press).

Index

370.15
ST 819

114 209